TAXcafe™

Taxcafe.co.uk Tax Guides

Grow Rich with a Property ISA

By Nick Braun PhD

Important Legal Notices:

TAXCafe˜
TAX GUIDE - "Grow Rich with a Property ISA"

Published by:
Taxcafe UK Limited
214 High St
Kirkcaldy KY1 1JT
Tel: (0044) 01592 560081
Email: team@taxcafe.co.uk

First Edition, March 2006

ISBN 1 904608 34 5

Disclaimer
Before reading or relying on the content of this Tax Guide please read carefully the disclaimer on the last page which applies. If you have any queries then please contact the publisher at team@taxcafe.co.uk.

About the Author & Taxcafe

Nick Braun founded Taxcafe.co.uk in Edinburgh in 1999, along with his partner Aileen Smith. As the driving force behind the company, their aim is to provide affordable plain-English tax information for investors, business owners, IFAs and accountants.

In the last five years Taxcafe has become one of the best-known tax publishers in the UK and received numerous accolades.

Nick has been involved in the tax publishing world since 1989 as a writer, editor and publisher. He holds a masters degree and doctorate in economics from the University of Glasgow, where he was awarded the prestigious William Glen Scholarship and later became a Research Fellow. Prior to that he graduated with distinction from the University of South Africa, the country's oldest university, earning the highest economics results in the university's history.

He went on to become editor of *Personal Finance* and *Tax Breaks*, two of South Africa's best-known financial publications before moving to the UK.

Nick and Aileen are very keen property investors and own a large portfolio of buy-to-let flats in the Fife seaside town of Kirkcaldy where the Taxcafe head office is based.

When he's not working Nick likes to take his children to the zoo, relax with friends and eat good food.

Dedication

Once again, to Aileen for all your love and support and to Jake, Sandy and Tilly for all the joy you bring.

Nick Braun, March 2006

Thanks

Thank you to my parents, Ann and Deryck, for all your encouragement over the years. I would also like to thank my in-laws, Douglas and June, for the tremendous help and support you have given us over the past five years.

Contents

Introduction

The Individual Savings Account or ISA is one of very few tax shelters available to private investors in the UK. The other main ones are pension funds, venture capital trusts and enterprise investment schemes.

ISAs don't enjoy as many tax breaks as other tax shelters – in particular, they don't give you an income tax refund when you put your money in.

However, what make ISAs more attractive than other tax shelters is their *flexibility*:

- **No minimum investment period.** Your investment returns are completely tax free whether you invest for one month or one decade.

- **Easy access to your money.** You can leave your capital invested and withdraw income tax free at any time or cash-in part of your investment and withdraw profits as a tax-free lump sum. Used this way, your ISAs can be both a tax-free savings vehicle or a tax-free income generator.

The ISA allowance was supposed to fall from £7,000 to £5,000 but in the 2005 Budget it was announced that the £7,000 limit will be retained until April 5th 2010.

So this wonderful tax break has been given a welcome stay of execution and we've all got several more years to accumulate a nice little nest egg that will be permanently protected from the taxman's clutches.

Investors will be able to make investments as follows:

Tax year ended April 5th 2006	£7,000
Tax year ended April 5th 2007	£7,000
Tax year ended April 5th 2008	£7,000
Tax year ended April 5th 2009	£7,000
Tax year ended April 5th 2010	£7,000

This means single taxpayers will be able to shelter £35,000 over the next five years and couples will be able to put away as much as £70,000 (if you're reading this after April 5th 2006 these amounts are £28,000 and £56,000 respectively).

After that? Who knows, but it would be very surprising to see this important savings incentive scrapped.

With the exception of bank account products, ISAs fell out of favour following the stock market collapse of 2000 to 2003. Sheltering profits from the taxman became the least of investors' worries... just making a profit in the first place seemed to take a miracle.

Since 2003 the stock market has been rising steadily and share investment is finally coming back into vogue. Healthy profits produce unhealthy tax bills which means using ISAs has become important once again.

But ISAs aren't just for share investors. What many people don't realize is that ISAs can also be used to invest in certain types of *property*.

Property ISAs have been available for a few years now but have not received much attention from the mainstream financial media. As a result many investors are unaware of their existence.

Most investors are also unaware of some exciting developments that have taken place in recent months – in particular, the number of property investments that qualify for ISA inclusion has been dramatically increased.

In this guide I'm going to explain exactly how you go about investing in a property ISA, weigh up all their benefits and drawbacks and then take a detailed look at some of the investments available.

In the chapters that follow I'm also going to explore some other very important issues that will be of interest to anyone investing in ISAs, not just property investors.

Every year some of the leading investment magazines publish ISA supplements. Most contain a list of expert share and unit trust tips and background information on how ISAs work. The better guides also contain detailed performance tables to help you choose the best investment funds for your ISA wrapper.

However, over the years I have found that none of the articles published in newspapers, magazines or specialist ISA supplements answer the *really* important questions.

For example, instead of an ISA are you better off using your savings to invest in something else or pay off your mortgage? Should you use an ISA to save for future expenses such as a child's education, or is it better to leave your savings intact to provide tax-free retirement income? Should you use your ISA allowance to invest in shares, bonds, cash or property?

These are some of the questions to which I *personally* wanted concrete answers and hence I decided to do the research myself. The result is this guide and I hope it provides you with some interesting insights and helps you make more profitable investments.

What you will not find, however, are any specific investment recommendations.

I'm a bit of a cynic when it comes to investment tipping. Over the last 17 years as a financial writer, editor and economist I've read hundreds and hundreds of investment recommendations. I don't know anybody who has consistently delivered the goods.

For example, last year one very well-known investment magazine recommended a selection of unit trusts to its readers for inclusion in their ISAs. Over the next 12 months the average return from these funds was 20.6%, compared with 18.9% from the stock market as a whole.

Not bad, you might say. However, if you ignore the returns from just *one* of these funds, a highly speculative fund which invests in countries like Russia, Hungary and Poland, the average return was just 16%.

In other words, most investors would have done better by simply sticking their money into a basic tracker fund which mirrored the performance of the Footsie.

Applying the same reasoning to property, I've provided lots of information about some of the available property ISA investments but there are no specific recommendations – I leave the reader to decide where to invest – or whether to invest in a property ISA at all.

I also haven't clogged up the pages of this guide with investment performance tables. Although these are extremely useful, the information can mostly be obtained free online from websites such as Trustnet (www.trustnet.com).

Chapter 1 gets straight down to business and explains how property ISAs work. However, some readers may benefit from reading the appendix first. There you'll find some answers to frequently asked questions (FAQs) about ISAs and explanations of some of the terminology. It's very important information but a bit boring so I decided to stick it in the back!

Thank you for purchasing this guide and good luck with your investments.

Nick Braun, March 2006

Chapter 1

Introduction to Property ISAs

Many people associate ISAs with the stock market, and many people still associate the stock market with losing money. That's why the ISA tax shelter is nowhere near as popular as it was at the end of the 1990s.

Of course you don't have to invest your ISA savings in company shares. You can also put your money in a savings account (limited to £3,000 per year) or invest it in government bonds.

These investments are low on risk but also, as one would expect, low on reward.

What most people do not know is that you can also invest your ISA savings in *property*.

Property ISAs are available from some of the UK's most reputable investment companies such as Norwich Union, Standard Life, Scottish Widows, Invesco and New Star.

They're ideal for anyone wanting to invest in growth assets, while steering clear of the ups and downs of the stock market. They're also ideal for anyone who wants to maximize their investment income.

The benefits are potentially huge. You get to invest in what is unquestionably the country's most popular type of asset and you get to do it using what is arguably the cheapest and most flexible type of tax shelter.

So What Exactly is a Property ISA?

Let me start by explaining what I do NOT mean when I use the phrase 'property ISA'.

First of all, I do not mean buying actual bricks and mortar and sheltering them inside an ISA. Inland Revenue regulations prevent you from investing in 'real' or 'actual' property.

As you'll see later on, however, property ISAs have a number of advantages over traditional bricks and mortar investments and are therefore a useful addition to most well-balanced investment portfolios.

Secondly, when I use the phrase property ISA I am not talking about *residential* property. At present most property ISAs are commercial property investments.

That's not necessarily a bad thing since commercial property has been the top-performing investment in the UK in the last couple of years. While residential property prices have drifted sideways, commercial property has enjoyed a boom period with a flood of money pouring into the market from big institutions and small private investors.

I have seen one or two property ISAs with a residential property 'flavour' but these are not widely available at present. I'll return to residential property ISAs later in the guide.

Thirdly, it's also important to point out that property ISAs are not investments in general property companies.

If you look at the share listings in any quality newspaper such as the *Financial Times* you'll see a category called 'Real Estate' and a category called 'Construction & Building Materials'.

Under these headings you'll find over 100 companies including estate agents, construction companies, home builders and other organisations providing property services. Examples include the likes of Savills, Balfour Beatty and George Wimpey.

Some of these companies have been spectacular investments during the property boom of recent years. For example, Savills has seen its share price rise from approximately £1.15 in 2003 to over £11 in March 2006.

In fact you could say investing in companies that make a living out of property is a better bet than investing in property itself. I don't know about you, but I'd much rather have invested in Savills shares a few years ago than bought any investment property from them.

As the old saying goes, it wasn't the prospectors who made the money in the Yukon gold rush, it was the people selling them picks and shovels!

It's possible to put all these 'Real Estate' and 'Construction & Building Materials' companies in an ISA and protect yourself from income tax and capital gains tax.

Despite the stellar returns of some property companies in recent years it's not these investments I'm referring to when I talk about property ISAs.

Although property company shares have performed extremely well in recent years there is no getting away from the fact that they are fundamentally a lot more risky than investing in property itself.

For example, Savills shares may have rocketed in recent years but the flipside is that they lost over half their value between 2001 and 2003. The Savills share price fell from around £3 in 2001 to under £1.50 in 2003.

Clearly property company shares are much more volatile and risky than property itself.

Property Investment Funds

When I use the term property ISA I am referring specifically to property funds – commercial property funds to be more precise.

These are *indirect* property investments. In other words, the investors don't own the property itself. Instead they own units or shares in a fund which owns property.

Property funds are the purest form of property that can be held inside an ISA. They're the next best thing to investing in property directly.

The fund takes your money and sticks it directly into shopping centres, retail parks, offices and warehouses. This produces a steady and predictable flow of rental income, most of which is paid out to investors.

I'm amazed how few people know that you can use your ISA allowance to invest this way, given the enormous interest in all things property and the thousands of column inches devoted to the subject in newspapers and magazines.

Property funds are attractive investments in their own right, even without the tax benefits of an ISA. Putting the two together produces a unique investment opportunity.

There are many pros and cons to investing in a property ISA. I'll be taking a very close look at ALL the benefits and drawbacks in the next two chapters. After that I'll take a closer look at the different offerings available.

Before we do that it's important to explain in more detail how these investments work.

Some of these funds are structured as property unit trusts, others as investment companies which are listed on the London Stock Exchange.

Property unit trusts have been around for many years and some, such as the £2 billion Norwich Property Trust, have delivered returns of over 15% per year. Despite being a fantastic way to invest in property, property unit trusts were only allowed into ISAs at the beginning of 2006.

For those who don't know, a unit trust is simply a financial product which pools money from a bunch of investors and uses it to buy a big spread of investments such as shares, bonds or property. Each investor holds units in the fund and the money is looked after by a professional fund management company which charges a small annual fee.

A *property* unit trust simply pools together money to buy lots of property: offices, high street shops, shopping centres, warehouses and factories. For a small initial investment of perhaps £1,000 the investor ends up owning a little piece of dozens of quality properties.

You'll find most property unit trust prices quoted in the *Financial Times* or on certain investment websites such as Trustnet.com.

And what about property investment companies? Until a few months ago the only way to invest in property through an ISA was to invest in one of these companies – the ISA rules state that shares in any company listed on any recognised stock exchange can be put in an ISA.

Investment companies are very similar to unit trusts except they're listed on the stock market. This means the investor owns shares instead of units. Although they're listed on the Stock Exchange they're a lot less volatile than 'conventional' share investments. The share price movements are much more closely correlated to the property market than the rest of the stock market.

You'll find 'Investment Companies' at the bottom of the share listing pages in the *Financial Times*.

An Example Fund

Chapter 6 takes a detailed look at some of the property funds that are open to private investors like you and me.

In the meantime let's take a very quick look at just one of the funds on offer so you have some idea what a property ISA actually looks like.

Take, for example, the UK Property Income Trust, managed by Invesco, part of the massive Amvescap group.

This fund has a portfolio of 47 properties worth around £300 million and dotted around most of England. A high proportion of the portfolio (46%) is invested in industrial property, with 40% in offices and 14% in shops and shopping centres.

The fund is structured as a Jersey-domiciled investment company listed on the London Stock Exchange

One of the fund's most valuable assets is a £12 million office park in Theale called Forum 1. To see this building go to this web page:

www.taxcafe.co.uk/exampleproperty

The fund manager spends his days looking for new properties to invest in and selling properties that are under-performing. When he's not doing that he'll be managing the existing portfolio: finding new tenants and negotiating new leases with existing ones.

For these services Invesco receives an annual fee – 0.85% of assets under management.

Rents are collected and then paid out to investors as dividends. At present this fund pays an income of 6.75 pence per share. When you consider that shares in the fund cost 128 pence each the 'rental yield' is 5.3%.

If you invest in the fund through an ISA that 5.3% income will, of course, be completely tax free. Because many property investors pay 40% income tax on their rental profits that 5.3% is equivalent to earning 8.8% outside an ISA.

In other words, if you invest in commercial property outside an ISA you will have to earn an 8.8% rental yield to beat a fund like this held inside an ISA.

It's also critical to point out that 8.8% is *net of all costs*: interest on borrowings, management fees and so on.

A net rental yield of this magnitude is almost unheard of in the world of buy-to-let flats.

Every few months the portfolio is revalued and when these figures are published this will cause the shares to move up or move down. The fund has achieved respectable capital growth since its launch just 18 months ago with the shares rising by over 20%. This capital gain will be completely tax free inside an ISA.

The fund is not involved in any risky activities such as property development, estate agency or land trading. It simply looks after a portfolio of buildings on behalf of investors such as you and me.

It is, however, allowed to borrow money to buy extra property and boost its rental income and capital growth. Most property investment companies have approximately 30-40% gearing. Property unit trusts do not have any borrowings.

If you want to buy shares in a fund like this all you have to do is phone up a stockbroker and you'll own them in minutes. However, to get the tax relief you have to buy them through an ISA, typically a self-select ISA.

A self-select ISA is essentially a 'do-it-yourself' ISA, available from most major stockbrokers and other investment companies. They allow you to invest your money pretty much as you please (see Chapter 9 for more information on self-select ISAs).

Summary

- Property ISAs are not investments in 'direct property' or bricks and mortar.

- Property ISAs are investments in property unit trusts and property investment companies.

- These funds invest directly in commercial property. The properties earn rental income which is paid out to investors.

- A typical property ISA will invest in a spread of commercial properties dotted all over the UK.

- A typical spread consists of shops, offices and industrial property. Some funds focus more on a specific sector, such as London offices or industrial properties.

- Some of these funds deliver an income of approximately 5.4% per year. Because ISA income is tax free this is equivalent to earning 9% outside an ISA, net of all property costs. Very few bricks and mortar properties have *net* rental yields of 9%.

- All capital gains are completely tax free. Some funds have delivered growth of over 15% per year.

In Chapter 3 I'm going to take a very detailed look at the benefits of investing in a property ISA. This is one of the most important chapters in the guide.

But before you read that chapter I suggest you carefully digest the contents of the chapter that follows.

It's essential for *anyone* who invests in ISAs, not just property ISAs and explains how you can maximize your ISA tax savings.

Chapter 2

Making the Most of the
ISA Tax Shelter

Introduction

ISA investors don't have to pay any income tax on their interest or dividend income, including income distributions from property funds, and they don't have to pay any capital gains tax on their profits.

In the best case scenario, this means you can protect up to 40% of your returns from the taxman.

In the worst case scenario, however, your ISAs will not save you one penny in tax.

How much tax you save depends on *how much* you invest, *how long* you invest for and *what type* of investments you make.

It's important to stress that very few people ever have to pay as much as 40% capital gains tax. This is thanks to two major reliefs:

- Taper relief, and

- The annual capital gains tax exemption

Taper relief generally protects between 5% and 40% of your profits from tax if you've held an asset for between three and ten years. 'Business assets', including many commercial property investments, are 75% tax free after just two years.

The taxable bit left over is then further reduced by the annual CGT exemption. The exemption is £8,500 per person for the 2005/2006 tax year and £8,800 for the 2006/2007 tax year.

The only investors who pay 40 per cent tax, therefore, are those who haven't held their assets long enough to get taper relief *and* who have already used up their annual CGT exemptions *and* are already in the top tax bracket.

Other investors will pay something between 0% and 40%, depending on their personal circumstances. For example, a couple who earn profits of £30,000 over three years will pay around 15% tax *at most*. A single person who makes the same amount of money will pay 26% tax at most.

And what about investment income? ISAs are ideal income tax shelters because:

Income is usually taxed more heavily than capital gains.

Take rental income as an example. Unlike capital gains tax there aren't any reliefs or allowances to protect you. Higher-rate taxpayers normally pay the full 40% tax on their rental profits and basic-rate taxpayers normally pay 22% tax.

Clearly, therefore, anyone who wants to earn rental income has a lot to gain by investing in a property ISA because all income distributions will be completely tax free.

What about share dividends?

Share investors receive dividends, the tax treatment of which can be extremely confusing thanks to terminology like 'tax credit', 'net dividend' and 'gross dividend'.

In practice it's quite simple: higher-rate taxpayers pay 25% tax on their cash dividends (the cheque you receive in the post). Basic-rate taxpayers pay no tax on their cash dividends.

So if you have shares or investment funds which produce a good income and you're a higher-rate taxpayer, you will save income tax by investing in an ISA. If you're not a higher-rate taxpayer, you won't save any income tax.

And what about interest income?

If you put your money in a bank account or in corporate or government bonds, most of your returns will be in the form of taxable interest.

Again there aren't any reliefs or allowances to protect you. Higher-rate taxpayers normally pay 40% tax on their interest and basic-rate taxpayers normally pay 20% tax.

In summary, anyone who wants to earn interest or rental income, or even dividend income, will benefit proportionately more by investing in an ISA, especially those who are 40% taxpayers.

Summary so far

Clearly how much tax you pay on your investments depends on a variety of factors:

- **What *type of investments* you own.** Assets which produce mostly capital gains are taxed *proportionately* less than assets which produce income. And some types of capital gains, such as those from business assets, are taxed more leniently than others.

- **How *long* you hold your investments.** Assets such as shares and property which produce capital gains qualify for taper relief if they've been held for more than three years (the holding period is less for business assets).

- **Your tax bracket.** Investment income and capital gains are added to your other income and this will determine whether you pay tax at 10%, 20%, 22% or 40%.

- **Your *marital status*.** Married couples each qualify for an annual capital gains tax exemption and can therefore earn profits of £17,600 during the tax year which starts on April 6th 2006, without paying a penny in capital gains tax. It's also possible for a working spouse to transfer assets to a non-working spouse thereby lowering the tax rate to either 20% or 10%.

- **How much *profit* you make.** Those with big investment holdings are far more likely to have profits which far exceed the annual capital gains tax exemption and will therefore end up paying more capital gains tax.

It's important to have a good understanding of how different investments are taxed and why your tax bill depends largely on your personal circumstances. Having this knowledge will help you maximise your ISA tax savings.

It would be a shame to waste your ISA allowance on investments that are already largely tax free in your personal circumstances. Far better to use it to shelter investments which will be most heavily taxed.

Saving for Future Expenses

Many investors use ISAs to save for future expenses. For example, you may wish to accumulate funds to pay for something important like a child's university or private school education, or something fun like an overseas trip.

Saving for future expenses implies that you plan to *cash in* your ISAs at some point in the next, say, three to ten years.

At first glance this seems like a perfectly sensible strategy. In reality, it could be the worst possible way to use your ISA allowance, especially if you are investing in assets which are normally subject to capital gains tax, such as property funds. In many cases, you will not save one penny in tax.

Example

Gordon and Sarah invest £5,000 directly in a property unit trust (note, *not* an ISA) to help pay for their son's future university fees. Let's say they earn 7% per year for 10 years and end up with a profit of £4,800 after selling their units.

These profits will be completely tax free because they're covered by the couple's annual capital gains tax exemptions.

So if Gordon and Sarah invested in the same unit trust *but using an ISA wrapper instead*, they would not save one penny in tax.

What if the couple invested much more money or earned a far higher return? Even in this situation an ISA may not be much use.

Example again

Let's say Gordon and Sarah invest £14,000 and earn an impressive 14% per year for 10 years. In this case they'll make a profit of £37,901 after a decade. Because they've held onto their investment for 10 years, 40% of these profits will be protected from the taxman by capital gains tax taper relief.

That leaves taxable profits of £22,741. However, we still haven't taken the couple's annual CGT exemptions into consideration.

The CGT exemption rises by at least £300 per year so in 10 years time it will probably be worth at least £11,000, or £22,000 for a married couple.

Therefore, of Gordon and Sarah's remaining £22,741 profits, only £741 is taxable. The total tax bill will be no more than £296.

In summary, Gordon and Sarah have invested without an ISA, made profits of £37,901 and paid just £296 in tax!

Where does this leave ISAs? Clearly an ISA wouldn't have been much use to Gordon and Sarah. They invested a sizeable chunk of money, earned a very high return and ended up paying barely any tax.

There are, however, situations in which investors *will* end up paying tax and will therefore benefit from using an ISA. The maximum tax savings are achieved when you use your ISAs for:

- Income
- Share trading
- Lump sum investment
- Regular savings
- Investing in bonds

ISAs for Income

Arguably the best thing to do with your ISAs is never sell them because, once you do that, the tax savings are lost forever. A better idea is to hold onto them and use the money to generate *tax-free income*.

Example

Gordon and Sarah invest £14,000 for 10 years in a growth ISA and enjoy returns of 7% per year. This time, however, the investment will not be cashed in and will, instead, be used to generate income.

After 10 years the investment will be worth £27,540 and they can switch tax free from the growth fund to an income-focused fund (ISA supermarkets, for example, let you invest in different funds provided by different managers and switch from one to the other at low cost).

If the income fund has a yield of 6% this will produce a tax-free income of £1,652 per year.

Now let's introduce William and Kate. They invest the exact same amount as Gordon and Sarah but, instead of using an ISA, invest *directly* in growth assets, such as shares or property.

When they switch their funds ten years later from growth investments to income producing assets, there will also be no capital gains tax payable. Their profits will be easily covered by taper relief and their annual CGT exemptions.

However, that's not the end of the story. When the income fund starts paying out, the full amount will be subject to *income tax*, possibly at the rate of 40%.

This will leave them with an after-tax income of just £991.

In other words, by using an ISA Gordon and Sarah end up with almost 67% more income than William and Kate.

What's more, these tax savings will be enjoyed by the couple *every year*.

Clearly ISAs are a fantastic way of accumulating savings to generate income.

ISAs for Share Traders

If you earn only average returns on small sums of money invested in the stock market, an ISA will possibly not deliver any tax savings at all. Most of your profits will be tax free anyway thanks to your annual capital gains tax exemption.

If, however, you have exceptional stock picking skills an ISA will deliver enormous benefits.

Example

George invests £14,000 in Elgoog a new internet search engine taking the world by storm. The shares rise 200% during the year and he makes a £28,000 profit. He now has £42,000 to invest and we'll assume he invests all his money in Oohay, another hot internet stock, and doubles his money. His profit this time will be £42,000.

His total profits are £70,000 and his total tax bill, after deducting the annual CGT exemption, is £24,480.

If George had invested through an ISA his total tax-free profits would be £70,000. Outside an ISA his after-tax profits are just £45,520.

In summary, ISAs are extremely valuable to skilled share traders and stock pickers.

It's worth pointing out, however, that share traders can also use spread betting as an alternative to an ISA. Spread betting profits are completely tax free but in certain circumstances are far more risky 'investments'.

ISAs for Lump Sum Investors

In the above example the investor earned a large return with a relatively modest initial sum of money. ISAs are also useful for investors who have built up significant savings and earn respectable but not incredibly high returns.

Example

Since ISAs were introduced James and Bev have accumulated £100,000 worth of savings. They invest in a property fund and earn a profit of £30,000 in just under three years. They then sell their investment.

Because they have invested through an ISA over the years their profits are completely tax free and they have the total amount of £130,000 to reinvest.

If they had invested *outside* an ISA the picture would not be quite as rosy. They could expect a tax bill of around £5,000.

They would then be left with just £125,000 to reinvest, compared with the £130,000 they managed to achieve inside an ISA.

Let's say they now invest their ISA savings in a brand new property fund for the next three years and earn 30% again.

Because their money is sheltered in an ISA their £130,000 will grow to £169,000 and there will be no tax payable.

Investing outside an ISA would have produced an entirely different outcome. Their £125,000 would grow to £162,500. Out of these profits they will have to pay a tax bill of roughly £7,500.

In total they get £169,000 investing with an ISA, compared with £155,000 without an ISA.

By sheltering inside an ISA, every time they take profits and switch into new investments they will have more money to reinvest and move further and further ahead of someone who invests outside an ISA.

In summary, ISAs are an excellent tax-saving device for anyone who has already managed to shelter significant capital inside one.

Most readers probably don't identify with the example of George, the share trader who magically doubles his money all the time, or James and Bev, who have managed to stash away £100,000 in ISAs already. I know I certainly don't.

The more interesting example was the first one, showing how ISAs can drastically increase your income.

The next example is also extremely relevant. It illustrates that if you use your ISAs as part of a regular long-term savings programme you will save a significant amount of tax.

ISAs for Regular Savers

If you haven't managed to accumulate significant ISA savings to date, don't worry, you still have four or five years to make up lost ground.

Up until 2010 a single person will be able to invest £7,000 every year and a couple will be able to invest £14,000 every year.

If you then hold onto your investment for several more years you could reap significant tax savings.

Example

Let's say Gordon and Sarah from the earlier example invest £14,000 *per year* for five years in a property ISA. They hold onto their investment for a further 10 years, hoping to build up a nice nest egg. We'll assume the portfolio grows by 8% per year.

At the end of the investment period the couple will end up with £191,503. Because they've used an ISA there will, of course, be no tax on their profits and the full amount will be theirs to do with as they please.

If they had invested *outside* an ISA there would be tax to pay, calculated as follows:

Profit	£121,503
Less:	
Taper relief @40%	£48,601
CGT Exemptions*	£25,400
Taxable Profit	£47,502
Tax @40%	£19,001
Capital remaining	£172,502

* An estimate of two CGT exemptions in 15 years' time.

So using an ISA in this instance has definitely been worthwhile as the couple will save approximately £19,000 in tax.

ISAs for Income Revisited

The example earlier under the heading 'ISAs for Income' showed that possibly the best thing to do with your ISAs is never cash them in. The biggest tax savings are often produced when you use them to generate tax-free income.

In that example Gordon and Sarah earned 67% more income because they sheltered inside an ISA.

That's an impressive result but they can still do better. Let's examine how much more income Gordon and Sarah earn by sheltering their regular savings from the above example in an ISA.

We've already shown that if they use an ISA they will end up with £191,503. They could then switch tax free into high-income assets paying 6% tax free – an income of £11,490 per year.

If they invest *outside* an ISA they will have only £172,502 to invest for income after paying £19,001 in capital gains tax. This will produce an income of just £6,210:

$$£172,502 \times 6\% \text{ income} - 40\% \text{ tax} = £6,210$$

In other words, by saving with an ISA they will end up with an income of £11,490. Outside an ISA they will end up with just £6,210.

Investing through an ISA produces 85% more income.

This example shows ISAs at their most powerful: when used to generate tax-free income.

None of our assumptions are implausible. All we've assumed is that a couple make full use of their ISA allowance for five years and earn a respectable return of 8% per year.

Investment in Gilts & Corporate Bonds

Most investment experts argue that bonds are an essential part of a well-balanced investment portfolio. You can invest in either corporate or government bonds (known as 'gilts' in the UK) and you can invest either directly or through a unit trust.

Bonds aren't very popular with the wider investing public although most of us have a lot of our pension fund savings in this type of asset. Bonds usually don't deliver as high returns as shares and property but government bonds are the safest investments around. In fact they're the only investment that can be described as *risk free*.

By risk free I mean you will always get all your money back if you hold your government bonds until they mature and you will always get all your interest payments.

The problem with these investments is most of the return comes as interest which is *fully taxed*. Share and property profits, on the other hand, are taxed much more leniently.

As a result, bond investors often end up with very low after-tax returns – often barely enough to keep up with inflation.

Example

Steve earns 4.2% interest from his UK Government bonds. Because he's a higher-rate taxpayer he pays 40% tax. This means his after-tax interest rate is just 2.5% – barely higher than UK inflation which is currently running at 2.4%. His savings are therefore only just keeping up with inflation but are not making him any more wealthy.

So while government bonds are risk free in some respects (you will always be repaid your original money and will always receive your interest payments) they can be high risk in other ways: because you have to pay a lot of tax on your returns your investment will at the very most keep pace with inflation.

This leads to the inevitable conclusion:

No investor should hold bonds unless there is some sort of protection from the taxman.

This is where ISAs come to the rescue. Because income is totally tax free, you are likely to earn a far more respectable return on your money and beat inflation comfortably.

Example

Paul and John invest £7,000 per year in corporate bonds for five years. John earns 5.5% per year but fails to invest in an ISA. As a result 40% of his returns end up in the taxman's coffers. Paul also earns 5.5% but invests in an ISA so his returns are tax free.

Both hold onto their investments for a further 10 years after making their initial contributions. How much better off is Paul from using an ISA?

The difference is stark. At the end of the investment period Paul will have savings of £70,403 whereas John will only have £53,436.

In other words, Paul the ISA investor has 32% more money than John. Clearly if you are investing in bonds you should consider putting your money in an ISA.

Summary

- Saving for future expenses, such as a child's education, is possibly the worst way to use your ISA allowance, especially if you are investing in growth assets such as shares. In many cases you will not save one penny in tax.

- Possibly the best thing to do with your ISAs is never sell them – instead use your savings to generate tax-free income. You could end up with almost 85% more income than someone who invests outside an ISA.

- ISAs are perfect for share traders who make big capital gains from year to year. Share traders don't qualify for taper relief because they only hold their investments for short periods of time and, if successful, their profits are likely to exceed the annual capital gains tax exemption.

- Investors who have managed to shelter significant savings over time within an ISA can reap big tax savings even if their investment returns are quite modest.

- If you invest your entire allowance each year and hold your investments for a reasonable period of time you will also save a significant amount in tax by using an ISA.

- If you invest in assets that earn interest, such as bonds or cash, you will also achieve significant tax benefits from an ISA.

- If you want to invest in property to earn rental income you could also be a lot better off going the ISA route, as the next chapter will make clear.

Chapter 3

Property ISAs: The Benefits

"A professionally managed, broadly diversified, liquid property portfolio, available for lump sum investments of only £1,000 is totally different from a single, speculative, and often highly geared, property asset." Gerardine Davies, manager of the £2 billion Norwich Property Trust.

Property has made a lot of people very wealthy in the last 10 years or so. With prices rising by over 20% per year in some parts of the country, anyone who borrowed to the limit and went on a spending spree will have made hundreds of thousands of pounds in profit... if not millions.

However, those heady days of double digit returns are arguably over and the 'easy money' has already been made.

Nevertheless property remains an extremely attractive investment. If you buy real estate in the right location and at the right price it will grow in value over the years and the rental income will grow with it.

You won't get rich quickly but you will grow rich *over time*.

During the next few years, as the feeding frenzy of the buy-to-let boom dies down, there will probably be major changes in the way people invest in property. In particular, there is likely to be a surge of interest in *indirect* property investment.

Whereas direct investment involves owning actual bricks and mortar, indirect investment means buying shares or units in a fund that owns the property. That fund will be something like a unit trust or company listed on the stock market and run by a reputable financial institution.

Real estate investment trusts in the US are a good example of the popularity of indirect property investment. This multibillion-dollar industry allows people to invest easily in shopping malls, offices and apartment blocks all over the country.

REITs address many of the problems of direct property ownership: they provide you with risk diversification (a big spread of properties), liquidity (you can buy and sell whenever you want) and expert management (property professionals who hunt down the best deals and squeeze as much rental income out of the properties as possible). Property ISAs offer many of the benefits of REITs... plus some mouth-watering tax breaks!

In the next two chapters I'm going to take a detailed look at all the benefits and drawbacks of investing in a property ISA. We'll start in this chapter with the advantages and move onto the disadvantages in Chapter 4. Then in Chapter 5 we'll take a detailed look at a case study comparing returns from the two types of investment.

Finally, it's important to stress that there is no right or wrong way to invest in property, only what works well for YOU. Furthermore it's not an all-or-nothing decision. You can invest some money in a property ISA and some in traditional bricks and mortar.

Property ISAs offer both tax benefits and non-tax benefits. In my opinion the non-tax benefits are just as important. Let's now take a closer look at some of them.

Advantage #1
Tax-Free Rental Income

Many investors are attracted to commercial property by rental income considerations. This type of property usually provides a far more reliable income stream than residential buy-to-let.

Most residential leases are of very short duration and tenants are usually private individuals, sometimes with little financial standing.

Commercial property leases usually last for several years (five to 10 years) and your tenants could very well be big blue-chip companies with a fairly low risk of going bust and failing to pay the rent.

Furthermore, by investing in commercial property through an ISA your income will be completely tax free.

And because ISAs are such flexible investments you can either reinvest this income or spend it immediately!

It's on the income tax side that property ISAs deliver some of their biggest tax savings. This is because many people pay the full 40% tax on their investment income and, unlike capital gains tax, there are very few reliefs or allowances to reduce the sting.

Exactly how valuable is the ISA tax break to property investors?

The simplest way to look at it is to compare after-tax rental yields from property held inside an ISA with property held outside an ISA

If you can get 5.4% income from a property ISA, you have to earn 9% from a direct property investment to end up with the same after-tax income.

It is virtually impossible to find any property with such a high *net* rental yield.

Looked at differently, if your property investment pays you an after-tax income of £6,000 per year, you could have earned £10,000 if the same investment was held inside an ISA.

If you can earn £6,000 outside an ISA and an extra £4,000 inside an ISA, that means:

ISAs give you 67% more income than other investments.

A more sophisticated way to compare property held inside an ISA with property held outside an ISA is to look at the long-term position with *rental income being reinvested year after year.*

Remember ISA investors can reinvest their income tax free whereas other property investors can only reinvest their after-tax income. This can make a big difference over a period of many years.

In fact, one of the drawbacks of traditional property investing is that it is very difficult to reinvest your income at all.
For example, if you own a small shop which pays you an income of £1,000 per month you will find it very difficult if not impossible to immediately reinvest that money in new property.

A major benefit of investing in a property ISA, or any investment fund for that matter, is that it's relatively easy to reinvest your income. This is because the minimum investment is often just a few hundred pounds and many funds have an automatic reinvestment facility.

And reinvesting income over a long period of time can have a significant effect on your overall investment returns.

Example 1

John, a higher-rate taxpayer has ISA savings of £20,000. Let's say he invests these in a property ISA and enjoys capital growth of 5% per year and income of 5% per year.

If he reinvests the tax-free income, after 10 years he will have an investment worth around £52,000.

If instead he invests in property outside an ISA he will have to pay tax on his rental income distributions and will therefore have less left over to reinvest. In fact his £20,000 initial investment will grow to just £43,000.

This example shows how ISAs are powerful wealth accumulators.

Example 2

John now decides to start spending his investment income. Because his money is in an ISA he can pay himself a tax-free income at any time. In this case his income will be:

£52,000 x 5% = £2,600

If he had invested outside an ISA his income would be:

£43,000 x 5% less 40% tax = £1,290.

The ISA produces over twice as much income after ten years!

This example shows how ISAs are also powerful income generators.

Advantage #2
Tax-free Capital Growth

When you sell shares in a property ISA you don't have to pay one penny of capital gains tax (CGT).

If you sell a property held *outside* an ISA there will most likely be capital gains tax to pay. The size of this tax bill will depend on a variety of factors:

- Whether your tenant is a 'quoted' company, in other words a stock market company

- How much income you've earned during the year, and

- Whether you've used up your annual CGT exemption.

Quoted vs Unquoted Tenants

If your tenant is an *unquoted* company (in other words, does NOT have a stock market listing) you will qualify for what's known as business-asset taper relief. This means 75% of your profits will be *completely tax free*, as long as you've owned the property for more than two years.

It's one of the most generous tax reliefs available to UK investors.

If your tenant is a quoted company, however, you will only get the less generous non-business asset taper relief. This means between 5% and 40% of your profits will be tax free, depending on how long you've held onto the property.

Most residential property only qualifies for this type of taper relief.

Clearly if you've owned property that qualifies for the more generous business asset taper relief you will not enjoy huge capital gains tax savings by investing in an ISA because most of your profits would be tax free anyway.

How Much Income You Earn

How much income you earn is important for capital gains tax purposes because, after deducting various reliefs and allowances, the taxable portion of your profit is added to your other income.

If you're already paying tax at 40% then all your taxable profits will be taxed at 40%. If you're a basic-rate taxpayer then some or maybe all of your taxable profits will be taxed at just 20%.

The benefits of an ISA will be felt most by those in the top tax bracket.

The Annual CGT Exemption

The annual capital gains tax exemption is £8,800 for the tax year starting on April 6th 2006 (£8,500 for the previous year).

Everyone gets an annual capital gains tax exemption which means married couples can enjoy tax-free profits of £17,600 per year.

Clearly the benefits of investing through an ISA are drastically reduced if 75% of your profits are tax free thanks to business taper relief and the remaining 25% is protected from tax by the capital gains tax exemption.

Example

Clare and Martin accumulate £28,000 of ISA savings over two years and decide to invest in a spread of commercial property funds. Let's say the funds enjoy capital growth of 7% per year. After 15 years the investment will be worth £77,253 and they can cash in the whole lot tax free.

But what would have happened if they had invested outside an ISA, for example, in some sort of property partnership?

If the property had *unquoted* tenants, three quarters of Clare and Martin's profits would be completely tax free thanks to business asset taper relief. The remaining taxable profits would be easily covered by their annual CGT exemptions.

In other words, they would not pay one penny of capital gains tax, despite investing *outside* an ISA.

Example 2

What if Clare and Martin invested in a property syndicate with a *quoted* company as tenant? After all most investors would prefer to rent their property to big stock market companies rather than small unknown ones.

In this case only 40% of their profits will be tax free and the remaining taxable profit will only be partially protected by their combined capital gains tax exemptions.

All in all they could expect to pay approximately £3,000 in tax.

Example 3

What if Clare and Martin have made maximum use of their annual ISA allowances and their initial investment is much higher, say, £70,000?

After 15 years their investment would be worth £193,132 and because it's held in an ISA there wouldn't be a single penny of capital gains tax.

If instead they'd invested in direct property with unquoted company tenants the tax bill would be £1,673 – pretty low when you consider that they've made a profit of over £123,000.

If, however, they'd invested in property with *quoted* company tenants the tax bill would be considerably higher: £18,912 to be precise.

Summary

- Property ISAs offer very few capital gains tax savings compared with commercial property let to unquoted tenants.

- Property ISAs offer reasonably attractive capital gains tax savings compared with residential property or commercial property let to quoted tenants, especially if you expect to make maximum use of your ISA allowance in the next five years.

Advantage #3
Very Low Stamp Duty

If you buy a commercial property costing between £250,000 and £500,000 you will have to pay 3% stamp duty. And if it costs more than £500,000 you will have to pay 4% stamp duty.

However, if you buy a property ISA the stamp duty is just 0.5% because you are buying trust units or shares rather than physical property.

If you buy £1 or £1 million worth of shares or units the stamp duty stays fixed at just 0.5%.

Although most commercial property costs more than £250,000 it's also worth pointing put that if you buy a property for *less* than £250,000 the stamp duty will be just 1% and if you buy commercial property for less than £150,000 there is no stamp duty at all.

In my opinion this is a very minor issue and one that should not influence your investment decisions either way.

Advantage #4
Very Liquid Investments

This is an important advantage of property ISAs over traditional property investments.

The more liquid an investment is the better. Most property is extremely illiquid because you cannot sell it quickly, unless you accept a drastic drop in price.

Property ISAs do not suffer from this problem. For example, shares in property investment companies can be sold within minutes by phoning your stockbroker or clicking a mouse if you have an online share dealing account. Unit trusts can also be cashed in quickly by contacting the fund management company in question.

In my opinion liquidity is a very important consideration -- just ask anyone who has struggled for many months to sell a buy-to-let property.

While you wait for a buyer you have to pay mortgage interest, council tax, insurance and other running costs and will probably not be earning a penny in rental income.

Direct property is also illiquid in the sense that you cannot sell it off in chunks. For example, you would struggle to sell 20% of a buy-to-let flat but you would not struggle to sell 20% of your shares or units in a property ISA.

There may be any number of reasons why you would prefer to sell part rather than all of an investment.

The ability to sell off your investment in chunks is also extremely useful if you're investing without the protection of an ISA.

By selling off small parcels of shares or unit trusts each year, investors can make use of their annual capital gains tax (CGT) exemptions much more readily than direct property investors.

For the 2006/2007 tax year the exemption is worth £8,800 per person or £17,600 if you're a married couple.

Very few direct property investors can make use of their CGT exemption every year because the costs incurred buying and selling property are too prohibitive.

Example

Lee has shares which have made a profit of £16,000. Instead of selling them all in one go he decides to sell half his holding at the end of the current tax year and the remaining half at the beginning of the new tax year. As a result all of his profit will be tax free because the first £8,000 in profit will be covered by this year's annual CGT exemption and the second £8,000 will be covered by next year's annual exemption.

If Lee owned a property with a £16,000 profit he would most likely have to sell the whole asset in one go. The first £8,800 would be covered by his annual CGT exemption. The tax bill on the remaining £7,200 could be as high as £2,880.

Advantage #5
Big Spread of Properties

This is without doubt one of the major attractions of property ISAs over direct property investment.

Commercial property is usually a lot more expensive than residential property so most investors cannot afford to invest in a broad range of sectors and in a broad range of geographic locations.

In fact most residential property investors also cannot afford to spread their risk by buying lots of different properties in different locations.

Investors in property ISAs do not face this problem. Putting your money in a property investment fund means you can invest in a property portfolio worth, say, £300 million with assets spread all over the country and divided amongst shops, offices and industrial units.

Just imagine owning part of a £10 million office block in the centre of London, a £15 million shopping centre in Manchester and a £9 million industrial park near Birmingham... plus dozens more properties like these spread all over the country.

Spreading risk is usually not a top priority for most property investors. Many have huge sums of money tied up in just one or two properties.

It's usually only when problems arise that the investor wishes he hadn't put so many eggs into one basket.

For example, if you only own one property and cannot find a tenant for, say, 12 months that could cause you serious financial problems if you have a mortgage to cover or depend on the rent to pay your living expenses.

Having two properties doesn't make matters much better.

However, if you own a small share in dozens of properties – as property ISA investors do – you don't have to worry if one or two are empty for any length of time.

There are lots of other problems that may arise if a lot of your wealth is tied up in just one or two properties. Apart from rental voids there are literally hundreds of other factors – unknown at the time you purchase the property – that could have an adverse effect on the rental income you receive or the capital growth of the property.

For example, if the property is badly flooded it may be impossible to rent out for several months. If the property has structural damage which was not discovered when the survey was carried out this may cost thousands of pounds to rectify. If the area where the property is located goes downhill this will severely affect rental and capital values.

If you still think spreading your risk is not important you should heed the warning of one property big-wig whose story I read recently.

One of his buildings, a recently empty office block in London, had just been refurbished at considerable cost when the local council approved a big builder's plan to re-develop the area.

This meant that the building could become the subject of a compulsory purchase order.

Such orders often take years to unravel and in the meantime the investor was left with a building that he could neither rent out nor sell.

He brought his story to the attention of readers of *Property Week* magazine:

"...Imagine if you were an investor owning only one building, which you hoped would provide you with a pension. It might represent your life savings. You bought it hoping that it would provide you with a good income then suddenly the rent tap is turned off."

Something like this could happen to anyone. However, in this case the building was just one part of a very big portfolio so the overall effect was minimal.

The lesson to be learned from horror stories such as this is: if you cannot afford to buy a big portfolio of properties one way of spreading your risk is to invest in a property fund.

Advantage #6
No Borrowings Required

Many experienced property investors argue that property itself is not a risky investment, it's the borrowing that goes with it that creates the problems.

Property ISAs only require a small outlay so no borrowings are necessary. You can invest as little as £100 in property funds whereas the minimum deposit alone on a direct property is usually 100 times that amount.

There are some investment companies promoting 'no money down' deals which do not require a deposit but, in my experience, these are difficult to arrange.

Because only small investments are required, ISAs are ideally suited to a regular monthly savings plan.

Furthermore, because most property investors have to borrow money to make a purchase this exposes them to a variety of risks:

Interest rate risk. If interest rates go up you may not be able to meet the cost of your borrowings out of your rental income which means you will have to rely on other income sources to pay your debt.

Rental voids. Residential property leases usually last for 12 months or less. This means your property stands a good chance of being empty for *at least* one month in 12. During these periods, which can last many months in areas swamped with buy-to-let property, you still have to find the funds to pay your mortgage and other expenses.

Commercial property leases usually last much longer but when a lease comes to an end it may take many months to find replacement tenants.

Reverse Gearing. If property prices fall your deposit will bear the full brunt of the fall. The following example illustrates this point.

Example

The Paltrows and the Therons each have £14,000 to invest. The Paltrows invest £14,000 in a property ISA, whereas the Therons use their money as a deposit on a small buy-to-let property costing around £94,000.

Property and share prices fall by 5%. How much does each couple lose? The Paltrows total investment is just £14,000 so they lose 5% of their money which is just £700. The Therons total property investment is £94,000 so they lose £4,700 which is a whopping 33% of their personal money (their deposit).

Although we have all become accustomed to property prices rising, any drop in asset values would hit property investors with mortgages far harder than property ISA investors because of the heavy levels of gearing most property investors take on.

Advantage #7
Help in Troubled Times

ISA investments can help you in times of financial hardship. For example, if you lose your job you could use savings accumulated in an ISA to pay your bills for several months. Even if you don't need to draw on your savings, you can simply stop making any new investments and rest assured that your ISAs will provide no additional financial burden.

Direct property investment, on the other hand, usually depends on you being in tip-top financial health, even if your property is fully occupied.

Very few property investments are completely self-sufficient for the first few years – most require regular cash injections to pay unexpected bills. In fact, many property investors cannot even meet their mortgage payments out of their rental income, let alone all the additional expenses which may arise.

So if you lose your primary source of income, for example, if you're made redundant or your business goes bust, your property investments could continue to provide an unwelcome drain on your cashflow.

Advantage #8
Low Upfront Charges

Investors usually have to pay upfront charges when they invest in any kind of asset, be it property or shares.

The good news is that property ISAs have very low upfront charges – typically between 1.5% and 5%. Property unit trusts have higher upfront charges than shares in property investment companies.

Direct property upfront charges are far less predictable. They vary from investor to investor and between residential and commercial property.

There could be legal fees, survey fees, mortgage arrangement fees, mortgage interest payments prior to letting, refurbishment and decorating costs, furniture and white good investments and letting agent registration fees.

In total you could be looking at paying between 3% and 7% of the property's value in upfront charges.

So it would appear at first glance that the upfront costs of investing in property are just a bit higher than the upfront costs of investing in a property investment fund.

However, the important point to remember is that, as a percentage of your *personal investment* – your deposit – direct property upfront costs are much greater... more in the region of 30%.

The implication of this is that if you decide to sell your property soon after purchasing it, the costs are likely to eat up a large percentage of your personal stake in the property.

Furthermore, when you sell a property you also have to pay estate agent's fees and legal fees again which could easily come to an extra 2% to 3%. Property investment funds do not have significant exit costs.

Advantage #9
Low Ongoing Charges & No Hidden Costs

ISA investors have to pay annual fees of between 0.85% and 1.5% of the value of the properties under management.

Ongoing charges for direct property investments are far more variable and usually much higher.

The *predictable* costs include letting agent's fees, building and contents insurance and accountant fees.

The great thing about ISAs and most financial market investments is that there are absolutely *no hidden costs*. Direct property investors, on the other hand, face a plethora of hidden costs which could make a serious dent in their cashflow.

When you invest in buy-to-let property, for example, you hope that your rent will at the very least cover your mortgage charges, insurance and letting agent fees, leaving you perhaps with a small rental profit.

In reality what you may find is that your property and tenants make constant demands on your wallet.

These hidden costs are so great in number it's impossible to list them. Here are some of the most frustrating ones that I personally have had to pay for various properties in recent months:

- Repair creaking laminate - £90
- Damp proof walls - £1,500
- Replace washing machine after just 1 month - £200
- Emergency electrician - £60
- Reattach radiator to wall – £60
- Repair flood damage caused by tenant – £100 excess

In case you're wondering what's so frustrating about having to foot the bill for an emergency electrician, it was so that the tenant could enjoy the privilege of having someone flick the fusebox switch back on after the power tripped!

Personally, I find these extra costs the most exasperating aspect of investing in buy-to-let property. You want to strangle your surveyor for not spotting any faults before you bought the property, you want to strangle your tenant for being so careless with your property and you want to strangle your letting agent for using such expensive workmen!

There's a good chance these expenses will eat up all your rental profits unless you have owned the property for many years and your mortgage payments are now a small percentage of your rents.

If you ask any accountant who does tax returns for property investors he will probably tell you that almost all his clients who have bought rental properties in the last few years are making rental losses.

With commercial property it's slightly different. For example, many leases require the tenant to maintain the building and pay insurance costs. However, when push comes to shove you can be sure that your building will not be maintained to a satisfactory level by someone else.

Advantage #10
No Time Cost

Did I say that hidden expenses are the most exasperating part of property investing? I meant to say all the time it takes to manage them!

The point here is that *even if you use a letting agent* your property investments will probably still take up a lot of your time, especially if you're very ambitious and want to acquire a large portfolio of buy-to-let flats.

Letting agents are great at doing the mundane things like collecting rents but, in my experience, many are not very useful when you really need them.

Apart from all the day to day problems that you may get dragged into as a property investor, you will also have to draw up accounts which can be time consuming or expensive if you own lots of property.

In my opinion building a substantial property investment portfolio is not compatible with holding down a busy career or looking after a family.

As a property ISA investor you have no time cost to worry about. Just like anyone who buys shares in any listed company or invests in a unit trust you do not have to get involved in the day to day running of the company or fund.

You don't have to worry about problem tenants, ongoing maintenance, arranging insurance, drawing up annual accounts, or replacing faulty dishwashers. Once you've made the investment you can sit back and relax.

Advantage #11
Expert Management

If you invest in a property ISA you will also benefit from having an experienced professional manage your investment.

The fund managers who run these property portfolios have many years' experience and bring three major skills to the table:

- They have the expertise and information to scout out new properties offering above-average rental yields and the potential to deliver rental growth and capital appreciation.

- They have the skills to identify which sectors (for example, shops or offices) are likely to deliver superior returns and where in the country the best opportunities lie.

- They have the experience to negotiate new leases with tenants and ensure that every property produces the highest possible rental income.

Advantage #12
Enormous Flexibility

ISA investors can chop and change their investments according to where the best returns are to be found. For example, you could switch from one property ISA with a heavy weighting in retail shops to another fund with a bigger concentration of industrial property or offices.

You can do this without incurring any significant charges and without paying a penny in capital gains tax.

Direct property investors do not enjoy this amount of flexibility. If you own a flat in Manchester and you feel Manchester property prices are too high it could cost you an arm and a leg to sell up and buy a new property in, say, Birmingham.

You'll have to pay estate agent's fees and legal fees when you sell the Manchester property as well as capital gains tax on your remaining profits. Then when you buy the new property in Birmingham you will have to pay another round of legal fees, stamp duty and maybe all the other upfront costs listed earlier.

The following example reveals how incredibly expensive it can be to sell one property in a low-growth area and buy a new one in a property hotspot.

Example

Dawn feels the Edinburgh property market has peaked and decides to sell her flat for £150,000 so that she can reinvest the proceeds in Belfast. She bought the property for £100,000 three years ago. She paid for the property with a personal deposit of £15,000 and used an interest-only mortgage for the balance.

Her actual ownership of the property is therefore her £15,000 deposit plus her £50,000 profit which comes to £65,000.

She sells the property and after paying estate agent and legal fees of £4,000 and capital gains tax of £14,000 is left with just over £132,000 to invest in Birmingham.

After paying a fresh round of legal fees and other costs she will only have about £130,000 to invest. All in all she has lost almost 15% of her property in costs.

Her personal stake in the property is now just £45,000 (her original £15,000 deposit and the leftover profits of £30,000 after all taxes and selling and buying costs have been deducted.)

So by simply switching from one property to another she has lost over 30% of her own money!

In summary, if you invest in traditional buy-to-let property it is time consuming and expensive to shuffle your investments around and invest in new up and coming areas.

If you invest in a property ISA it is easy, cheap and tax free to shuffle your investments around and rebalance your portfolio.

Summary

Property ISAs offer the following benefits over direct property investments:

- **Tax-free rental income**. As a result ISA investors can easily earn 67% more income than direct property investors and possibly 100% more income.

- **Tax-free capital gains**. This benefit is probably less important than the income tax savings.

- **Liquidity**. Your investment can be bought or sold within minutes and sold off in small chunks.

- **Big spread of properties.** You will own a small share of dozens of office blocks, shopping centres and industrial parks, located all over the country.

- **No need for a mortgage.** Borrowing money is what makes property investment risky. In particular, a small drop in property prices could wipe out your personal stake in the property.

- **Help in troubled times.** You can sell your ISA savings quickly and use them to bail you out of financial difficulty. Traditional property investing requires you to be in tip-top financial health.

- **Low charges.** Property ISAs have low upfront charges, low ongoing charges and no hidden costs.

- **No time cost**. Property ISAs require virtually no time commitment from the investor, making them ideal for people with busy working lives or family commitments.

- **Expert management**. Property ISA portfolios are managed by experienced property professionals who scour the country for new properties and try and maximize the rental income from existing properties.

- **Investment flexibility**. Property ISA investors can sell existing investments and reinvest in alternative assets cheaply and without having to pay tax.

Chapter 4

Property ISAs: The Drawbacks

In the previous pages I've spent a great deal of time outlining the many advantages of property ISAs compared with direct property investments.

It's important to stress that these benefits do not necessarily provide a compelling case to go out and open an ISA.

As with every investment, property ISAs have their drawbacks too. Furthermore, direct property investment offers a number of opportunities that are not open to ISA investors.

Let's take a closer look at some of them.

Drawback #1
No Gearing Benefit

In the previous chapter I pointed out that many investors will like the fact that as an ISA investor you do not have to borrow any money to invest.

Because the minimum investment is so small – hundreds of pounds rather than hundreds of thousands of pounds – you are not obliged to borrow any money to get in on the action.

However, for many investors this will be seen as a major drawback because borrowing money is also the way to make big money in the property game.

Even rich investors borrow money to give their returns a boost. They call it 'leverage' because your returns obtain the same type of power as a mechanical lever.

Example

Jeffrey and Mary have £14,000 to invest. They use it as a deposit on a small flat costing £70,000 and borrow the rest of the money. Now let's assume the value of the property increases by a measly 5% per year over the next 10 years. We'll also assume that their rental income only covers the cost of their interest-only mortgage and their other letting costs – so all the couple are left with at the end of the day is the rise in the value of their property and their initial deposit.

After 10 years the property is worth £114,023. If they sell it and repay their £56,000 loan they'll be left with £58,023. What the couple have achieved, despite earning very modest returns, is to turn £14,000 into £58,023 in just 10 years. This means they have earned about 15% per year on their original money.

This ability to turn a 5% return into a 15% return is sometimes called the 'magic of gearing':

Even investments that earn modest returns can make you rich if you borrow money to invest in them.

As long as your investment returns exceed the cost of borrowing you will be OK.

There are, of course, risks involved if you borrow money to invest in property and these were outlined in the previous chapter.

However, this strategy has worked for many investors over the last few years. Thanks to easy lending criteria, low interest rates and a relatively strong rental market in many parts of the country, it has been relatively easy to borrow money cheaply and pay the cost out of rental income.

And with property having delivered double-digit capital growth, anyone who did this on a large scale will have made an enormous amount of money.

ISA investors simply cannot gear up their investments in this way. The maximum investment is £7,000 or £14,000 if you're a married couple.

In other words you will enjoy capital growth on only £14,000 while your property investor friends may be enjoying capital growth on at least five times as much property.

Although ISA investors cannot *personally* gear up their investments it's important to point out that some property funds gear up their portfolios using borrowed money. Listed property investment companies usually borrow money, property unit trusts do not.

This has helped property investment companies boost their returns considerably in recent years, though not to the same extent as buy-to-let investors.

Property investment companies typically have between 30% and 50% gearing. In other words for every £1 of equity they will have between 30p and 50p of borrowing. Buy-to-let investors usually have much more gearing. For every £1 of equity they will typically have at least £4 of borrowing.

So direct property investors who borrow more money *will* enjoy higher returns than property ISA investors... provided everything goes to plan: property prices rise *strongly*, rental income covers mortgage repayments and interest rates stay low.

However, as we will see in the next chapter, a property ISA investor could, in certain circumstances, earn a far higher return than a heavily geared buy-to-let investor.

Drawback #2
Property ISAs Can Be More Volatile than Direct Property

One of the things property investors hate most about the stock market is its horrendous volatility.

There's nothing worse than turning on the 10 o'clock news only to find out that 10% of your wealth has been wiped because some Third World country forgot to pay its credit card bill.

Stock market investments are subject to vicious price swings which do not affect those who invest in other assets such as property.

And there's no getting away from the fact that some property ISAs are stock market investments which means their prices can change daily.

As it turns out most property investment company share prices are somewhat removed from the day to day volatility experienced by other company share prices.

This is because earnings from property investment companies are extremely predictable because all they earn is rental income and much of that rental income is known for years into the future.

Earnings from other companies are much less predictable over long periods of time and based on, for example, how many units of software or cans of beer they can sell. Investment analysts find these numbers far more difficult to guess.

If you look at a graph comparing property company share price movements with the overall stock market you'll notice that the latter zig zags up and down much more.

Nevertheless, if a big market correction were to occur, for example if there was a major terrorist attack, you could see the share prices of property investment companies plummet, if only for a short while, until calm is restored.

It's important to stress that this problem does not affect those who invest in property unit trusts. These investments are not listed on the stock market and the price of the units is simply the price of the underlying properties.

Drawback #3
Discounts & Premiums

One of the biggest drawbacks of property investment companies is that their share prices can trade at a *discount* or a *premium* to their property assets.

At present most funds trade at a *premium* of between 5% and 10%. In other words you may end up paying £1.10 for £1 of property.

This does not apply to property unit trust investors. Unit trusts are much simpler to understand than investment companies. The value of a typical unit trust investment is simply the value of the investments it owns. Every day this is recalculated and the price is published in the major newspapers.

With investment companies it's not quite so simple. The share price is not a perfect reflection of the assets it owns.

When a property investment company is launched it raises money from investors, as does any company which decides to list on the stock market. Once the funds are raised the company becomes closed to new money.

That's why investment companies are also known as 'closed-end' funds, whereas unit trusts are known as 'open-end' funds because they can accept new money every day.

In the case of property investment companies the fund manager then goes out and buys a bunch of buildings. Although the investment company does not accept any new money you can invest in it by buying the shares. Remember the fund is listed on the stock market so anyone can do this.

Now for the important bit. Unlike a unit trust the price of investment company shares is not identical to the portfolio of properties it owns.

All share prices are determined by one thing and one thing only: investor demand. If lots of investors want the shares the price will rise and if lots of investors want to dump the shares the price will fall.

At any point in time the price of a company's shares could diverge wildly from the value of the assets it owns.

With property investment companies, although share prices are driven by investor demand, they usually do not diverge too much from the underlying net assets: the value of the properties.

This is because the company's earnings – its rental income – is extremely predictable from month to month so the markets rarely receive a nasty surprise which causes shares to be dumped and prices to fluctuate wildly.

However, if investors are particularly fond of a particular fund there will be extra demand for its shares and this may lead to the existence of a premium. In other words, to buy the shares you will have to pay more for the properties than they're worth. The premium is what you pay to get a good manager to look after your properties.

Similarly if a fund falls out of favour investors may start selling the shares aggressively and this may result in the creation of a discount. In other words, the shares are worth slightly less than the value of the underlying properties.

Discounts and premiums are a fact of life in the multibillion-pound investment trust and investment company industry and shouldn't cause you too much heartache.

It is, however, essential to know of their existence.

Although you may have to buy property company shares at a premium that doesn't necessarily mean that you will 'pay too much' for them.

The best known investment fund in the world, Berkshire Hathaway run by America's second richest man, Warren Buffett, has famously traded at a premium of around 100% for many years and investors keep piling into it.

The main thing that matters is not so much the existence of the premium but the likelihood that it will change into a discount (in other words, the share price will fall dramatically). This does happen from time to time.

It's important to reiterate that this drawback does not apply to investors in property unit trusts.

Drawback #4
Less Investment Choice

There's no getting around the fact if you want to invest in a property ISA your choices are fairly limited at present. There are only a dozen or so funds on offer.

However, all this is likely to change for the better in the months and years ahead.

The recent inclusion of property unit trusts in the list of qualifying ISA investments will probably encourage some fund management companies to set up new property funds.

As one property unit trust manager put it to me: "This must be an exciting development for UK private investors and will lead to heightened interest in property unit trusts.

"We are currently looking at the opportunities open to us ...Whilst we do not know full details yet, we are certainly investigating how we can take advantage of this change in regulation."

Property unit trust investors do not suffer from some of the problems experienced by investors in property companies.

For example, there is no discount/premium issue and because they are not listed on the stock market they're no more volatile than any other property investment.

Another exciting development expected within the next 18 months or so is the launch of the UK equivalent of US real estate investment trusts (REITs).

Nobody is entirely sure what these investments will look like. For example there is uncertainty as to how much money they'll be able to borrow and whether they'll be eligible for inclusion in an ISA (although it is expected that they will be).

All in all the future of indirect property investment, in particular property ISA investment, looks extremely promising.

Drawback #5
Limit of £7,000 per Year

Although ISA investors can invest very small amounts of money, the converse does not apply.

In other words, if you have a big lump sum you cannot invest in a property ISA – not in one go anyway.

The maximum annual investment is just £7,000 per person per tax year. Couples can therefore invest £14,000 per year.

Unlike buy-to-let investors, you cannot use your ISA investment as a down payment for a big loan and hence 'gear up' your returns.

So ISAs arguably do not provide a means of accumulating vast amounts of wealth.

Over time, however, it is possible to accumulate a significant amount of capital inside an ISA if you make full use of your annual allowance and your investments perform well.

Drawback #6
No Residential Property at Present

At present most property investment funds invest exclusively in *commercial property*.

This would have been perceived as a serious problem a few years ago when residential property was booming and commercial property was very much the poorer cousin.

Not so any more. With residential property moving sideways if not declining in some parts of the country, it is commercial property that is stealing the show.

Commercial property auction houses have been reporting record demand and prices have been rising strongly.

Some investors are calling it a bubble, others say there is so much demand from both big institutions and private investors that prices will continue to rise.

However, it's important to stress that commercial property is not cheap at present. If you invest in a property ISA now there is a danger that you are investing too late in the day.

There are no property investment funds which hold bricks and mortar residential properties. However, there are one or two funds which track residential property prices.

Take for example the CF Abbey House Price Plus Fund. This fund contains residential property derivatives and aims to beat the Halifax House Price Index over a period of three to five years.

Halifax House Price Index
All houses, all buyers
2003-2005

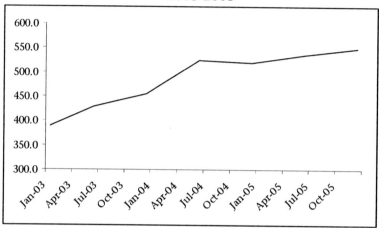

The fund can be put in an ISA and is available from Cofunds (www.cofunds.co.uk) for a minimum investment of £3,000.

The fund has an initial charge of 3% and an annual charge of 1.5%.

The Halifax House Price Index is one of the best known and reflects changes in property prices all over the UK. You can check it online at:

www.hbosplc.com/economy/housingresearch.asp

The Halifax produces lots of different measures. The one used for the Abbey fund is the "all houses, all buyers, non seasonally adjusted" index.

The graph above shows how this index has fared from 2003 to 2005. Although house prices in general have not crashed as many predicted, the index has not grown very much in recent times either, with annual house price inflation slowing to under 5%.

Also there was a small dip in the index from the middle of 2004 to around the middle of 2005 (in other words, you would have lost money during this period).

Drawback #7
No Genuine Bargains

One of the things I love most about property investment is that, unlike the stock market, genuine bargains can be had, provided you spend time acquiring the necessary local knowledge.

In other words, if you know what you're doing it's possible to find property selling for 'less that it should'.

This is rarely if ever possible with stock market investing. The stock market is a much more 'efficient' market than the property market. Being 'inefficient' makes the property market far more attractive to amateur investors.

Also, with property it's much more easy to become a leading expert in one small area (for example, one type of property in one particular location) and reap significant rewards as a result. Having such 'insider knowledge' is one of the keys to making profitable property investments.

If you invest in a property investment fund you are not going to be picking up a bargain or buying property at below market value. Any capital growth you enjoy will be due to a general rise in property prices rather than your skill at finding undervalued properties.

Chapter 5

ISAs vs Direct Property: Detailed Example

Introduction

It's clear from the detailed analysis in the previous two chapters that there are many differences between putting your money in an ISA and investing directly in property.

Some of the benefits of direct property investment will appeal to certain types of investors, while some of the benefits of indirect property ISAs will appeal to others.

For example, owning part of a large portfolio of properties will appeal to some investors; others would prefer to scout for property themselves in the hope of picking up a genuine bargain.

Some investors will like not having to be a landlord with all the responsibility this entails; others like the idea of investing in 'proper' bricks and mortar rather than property fund units or shares.

As I said before, there's no right or wrong way to invest in property – only what's right for you.

And it's not an all-or-nothing decision – you can invest in both property funds and direct property!

In my opinion, the two most important differences between property ISAs and direct property investments are the following:

- Property ISA returns are completely tax free.
- Direct property can be 'geared up' using borrowed money.

ISAs therefore have one major advantage and one major disadvantage: all returns are tax free but you cannot boost your returns using gearing.

Direct property investments also have one major advantage and one major disadvantage: you can gear up your returns using borrowed money but your returns are taxed.

For many investors not being able to gear up the investment would be seen as a serious drawback. When property prices are only rising slowly, as they are now, there are essentially only four ways to make money:

- Buy at a genuine discount and sell quickly – property trading.

- Buy, renovate cheaply and sell – property refurbishment.

- Buy with borrowed money and hope the small rise in property prices will translate into an attractive return thanks to gearing – the traditional buy-to-let model.

- Buy without borrowed money and reinvest your rental income – the property ISA route.

Property trading is quite difficult if you're a part-time investor and genuine opportunities only come along every now and again.

Property refurbishment can be very lucrative but takes practice. Furthermore, it's extremely time consuming. I would classify property refurbishment as a part-time job rather than an investment activity.

That leaves us with traditional buy-to-let and property ISAs.

The traditional 'buy-to-let' model is based on the principle that by borrowing lots of money you get to enjoy the capital appreciation on a much bigger chunk of real estate than you could otherwise afford.

The great thing is that even if property prices are rising very slowly you can still make good money out of traditional buy to let – what I call turning 5% per year into 15% per year.

There are risks involved, the most important one being that property prices might fall.

In these circumstances you will suffer from 'reverse gearing' and a relatively modest drop in property prices could wipe out most if not all of your original deposit.

The second major danger is that the property will lie empty and there will be no rental income to cover your mortgage and other expenses.

The final way of making money is to invest in a property ISA. This is arguably much less risky because no borrowed money is involved, and because there are no borrowings you get to keep all the income which you can either spend or reinvest.

Furthermore, this income and all your capital gains are completely tax free.

I described property ISAs as 'arguably' less risky because there are certain unique risks attached to this type of investment.

In particular, if you invest in a listed property investment company the share price could fall sharply if there is a sudden loss of confidence in the property sector. Financial assets tend to be more volatile than real assets.

So which investment is likely to deliver superior returns? If everything goes according to plan does heavy gearing generate more wealth for the investor? Or do the tax savings and income payouts enjoyed by property ISA investors produce greater returns?

The only way to answer this question is to follow two investors over a period of time, one investing in a property ISA, the other investing in traditional buy-to-let.

I think the results of this case study make fascinating reading.

Case Study – Carl & Isabel

Carl and Isabel each have £15,000 to invest.

Carl decides to put his money in a tax-free property ISA.

Isabel decides to use her money as a deposit for a £50,000 share in a commercial property and borrow the remaining £35,000.

The example is based on the following assumptions:

- Although the maximum ISA investment is £7,000 per year we can assume that Carl has already accumulated some ISA savings.

- Carl earns a combined return (income and capital growth) of 10% per year. This return is completely tax free inside an ISA. All income distributions are reinvested.

- Isabel enjoys capital gains of 5% per year. All of her rental income goes towards paying interest charges and other landlord expenses.

- Like many commercial property mortgages this one requires a 30% deposit.

Let's assume Carl and Isabel hold onto their investment for 10 years and then sell up and use their savings to generate income.

Carl and Isabel's After-tax Returns

After 10 years Isabel's share in the property will have grown by 5% per year from £50,000 to £81,445 – a profit of £31,445.

Carl's £15,000 grows by 10% per year to £38,906 (remember his property fund income is available for reinvestment because there are no borrowings).

Their investments are summarised in Table 1. At the beginning of the period Isabel, the direct property investor, has £50,000 to invest.

Table 1
Property ISA vs Direct Property

End of Year	Direct Property	Property ISA
1	52,500	16,500
2	55,125	18,150
3	57,881	19,965
4	60,775	21,962
5	63,814	24,158
6	67,005	26,573
7	70,355	29,231
8	73,873	32,154
9	77,566	35,369
10	81,445	38,906

All her rental income is eaten up by interest charges and other property letting expenses. However, she enjoys capital growth on a much larger chunk of property than Carl, the ISA investor.

After just one year her property investment has risen by 5% and is worth £52,500. Her investment grows nice and steadily in this fashion until after 10 years it is worth £81,445.

And what about Carl the ISA investor? At the beginning of the period he has just £15,000 to invest. However, his rental income does not get eaten up in loan repayments and other expenses. After one year he has enjoyed a 10% combined return equal to £1,500.

Isabel is doing much better at this stage – her capital gain in year one is £2,500 versus Carl's total return of £1,500. But Carl's investment is permanently sheltered from tax. Furthermore, Carl's higher combined returns eventually start to catch up with Isabel – this is the power of compound interest at work: he is reinvesting his rents and this money is generating further rental income and capital growth.

After 10 years Carl's property ISA is worth £38,906. It's clear that he has made up a fair bit of ground on Isabel. Ten years ago his property investment was one third the size of her's; now it is almost half as big.

Time to Sell Up

Carl and Isabel now decide to sell their property investments and put the proceeds into alternative high-income assets.

When Carl sells his property ISA there will be no capital gains tax so he will be left with the full £38,906.

What about Isabel? She has invested outside an ISA so when she sells up her profits will be subject to capital gains tax. How much tax she pays will depend upon:

- Whether the property has been let to quoted or unquoted tenants.
- Whether she is a 40% taxpayer.
- Whether she has already used up her annual CGT exemption.

I'll assume Isabel's property is let to high quality quoted tenants. This means she only qualifies for non-business asset taper relief and only 40% of her profits are tax free after 10 years (as opposed to 75% if she had unquoted tenants).

This assumption makes the example more relevant to residential property investors who also only qualify for non-business asset taper relief.

We'll also assume that Isabel is a 40% taxpayer but has not used up her annual CGT exemption.

So where does all this leave her after 10 years? She sells her property investment for £81,445 and the CGT bill is calculated as follows:

	£
Proceeds	81,445
Less: Original cost	50,000
Gain	**31,445**
Less: Taper relief	
40% x £31,445	12,578
Less: CGT exemption*	11,500
Taxable gain	7,367
Tax @ 40%	**2,947**

* The CGT exemption is assumed to grow to £11,500 over 10 years.

So from her £81,445 property sale we have to deduct £2,947 tax and, don't forget, £35,000 in borrowings to leave her with £43,498.

In summary, Carl the ISA investor ends up with £38,906 and Isabel the direct investor ends up with £43,498. So Isabel has managed to accumulate more wealth than Carl.

However, that's not the end of the story. What we must not lose sight of is the fact that:

- Isabel may have more money but she had to borrow money (take more risks) to get to where she is. Furthermore,

- Carl has less money but his savings are still inside an ISA and enjoying complete protection from the taxman.

Let's say Carl and Isabel put their money into income-focused investments and earn 5% per year. Because she is a higher-rate taxpayer Isabel will end up with:

£43,498 x 5% - 40% tax = £1,305

Carl, on the other hand, will not pay any income tax so his income will be:

£38,906 x 5% = £1,945

Carl the property ISA investor ends up with 50% more money than Isabel the heavily-geared property investor.

I find this result fascinating. Although borrowing money to invest in property is risky you would expect to earn superior returns if everything goes to plan.

In this case the ISA's tax benefits have ruled the day and turned a less risky investment into one that is more profitable as well.

This example shows that:

Having *less* money inside an ISA is often much better than having *more* money outside an ISA.

Like all examples a number of assumptions were made in obtaining the above result. None of these assumptions are all that unrealistic in my opinion but changing them will change the outcome. For example:

- **Rental profits.** I assumed that Isabel, the direct property investor, makes no rental profits over the whole 10 year period. You could argue that over time rents will rise but borrowing costs will probably remain static so a rental profit will emerge at some stage.

  Comment: This is true but many investment properties make a loss in the early years, something we did not inflict on Isabel in this example. Furthermore, managing a property portfolio is a time-consuming business, even if you use a letting agent. Time is money and so we could treat any rental profit as remuneration for Isabel's time.

- **Capital gains tax.** When Isabel sold her property we only gave her 40% taper relief whereas she would qualify for 75% relief if the property was a commercial one let to unquoted tenants.

  Comment: This is true but most property investors buy residential property which only qualifies for 40% taper relief. If Isabel enjoys 75% taper relief she will not have any capital gains tax to pay and her final income will be a bit higher (£1,363) but still far lower than Carl's.

- **Capital gains tax again.** Isabel won't have to pay any capital gains tax if she simply holds onto the property and uses it to generate rental income.

Comment: True but she'll still have to find a lump sum from somewhere to pay back her interest-only mortgage. Furthermore, no investment should be held indefinitely, including property. Investors should have the flexibility to sell and reinvest in more lucrative opportunities from time to time. Finally, even without any CGT we've just shown that her income will still be much less than Carl's.

- **Amount of borrowings**. Isabel only borrowed 70% in this example but most buy-to-let investors borrow about 80% to 85%.

  Comment: Increasing Isabel's borrowing will increase her returns but will also increase her risk.

- **Property price rises**. I assumed that property prices appreciate by just 5% per year. If they rise by more this will benefit Isabel who owns a larger chunk of real estate.

  Comment: This is the critical assumption. The more property prices rise the more Isabel will benefit because she owns much more property than Carl.

Example 2

Carl and Isabel are in the same situation as before except this time Isabel borrows an extra £25,000 to take her gearing to 80%. Furthermore, we assume that property prices rise by 7% per year instead of 5%.

However, we still assume that Isabel sells her property to pay off her mortgage and therefore ends up paying capital gains tax.

In this case Carl is still better off but only marginally. His ISA will produce a tax free income of £2,329 per year compared with Isabel's £2,242.

Again, Carl earns more money and has a much less risky investment!

Example 3

This time let's say property prices rise by 10% per year over the entire period.

Now Isabel's a bit better off than Carl. She ends up with a property investment worth £194,531 compared with Carl's property ISA which is only worth £60,683.

After paying capital gains tax and repaying her mortgage Isabel will enjoy an after-tax income of £3,313, compared with Carl's income of £3,034.

There are further adjustments we could make in favour of Isabel including giving her some rental profit and allowing her to hold onto the property instead of having to sell it and pay capital gains tax.

However, what the above examples show is that when property prices are rising only slowly, heavily geared and hence risky property investments may not perform much better than low risk property ISAs.

Chapter 6

Property ISAs Compared

Introduction

In the last few chapters we've taken a very detailed look at the benefits and drawbacks of investing in a property ISA. We've also taken a look at how these investments are likely to perform compared with traditional property investments.

Now it's time to take a closer look at some of the funds on offer.

In the following pages you'll find details of several property investment companies and property unit trusts offered by the likes of Standard Life, Invesco, Scottish Widows, F&C Asset Management, New Star and Norwich Union.

We'll take a look at what type of property the funds have bought and in what part of the country. Where possible I'll also list some of their biggest properties and how they split their money between shops, offices and factories.

You'll also find out how well each fund has performed in recent times and what sort of income yield you can expect.

Details are also provided of borrowing levels and the average duration of leases.

Each listing also contains contact details for the fund and how to find the share or unit price.

Please note that these are NOT recommendations to buy. Before you invest any of your money I suggest you have a chat with a suitably qualified financial adviser.

Before we go any further it's also worth briefly listing the benefits and drawbacks of property investment companies versus property unit trusts.

Property Investment Company Advantages

- **Can borrow money**. Property investment companies use gearing to boost their returns; property unit trusts do not borrow money. Borrowing money makes the investment more risky but can also lead to higher returns.

- **Lower charges.** Upfront and annual charges of property unit trusts are often twice as high as those of investment companies.

- **Higher income yields.** For a number of reasons property investment companies tend to have higher initial yields than property unit trusts.

- **Less cash in the portfolio**. Property unit trusts usually hold much more cash in their portfolios because they receive new money from investors every day. This could lower their returns slightly.

- **No property shares.** Many property unit trusts also invest in property shares. This makes them a bit more risky than property investment companies which usually stick to bricks and mortar investments.

Property Unit Trust Advantages

- **Not listed on the stock market**. For many investors, the fact that property investment companies are listed on the stock market is a distinct disadvantage. This means prices are potentially more volatile than direct property investments. Property unit trusts do not face this problem.

- **Automatic reinvestment of income.** An attractive feature of many unit trusts is that income can be automatically reinvested to buy more units. This can have a significant impact on your long-term returns. Investors in property investment companies can also do this but it's a bit more tricky in practice.

  Most unit trusts reinvest income automatically by offering what's known as accumulation units. The price of accumulation units is usually higher because reinvesting the income makes those units more valuable.

PROPERTY INVESTMENT COMPANIES

1. Invesco UK Property Income Trust

Introduction

The Invesco UK Property Income Trust was launched in September 2004 and has a portfolio of 47 commercial properties worth about £300 million.

The primary aim of the fund is to generate a *high income* for investors, as well as income growth and capital growth.

The fund's strategy is to invest in 'business space' properties, in particular industrial property and offices.

The fund is structured as a closed-ended Jersey domiciled investment company listed on the London Stock Exchange and Channel Islands Stock Exchange. You'll find the share price online if you go to Yahoo Finance (http://uk.finance.yahoo.com) and type 'IPI' in the share price lookup box.

Invesco is one of the UK's best-known fund management companies and part of the massive Amvescap group.

Share price: 128p (a 12% premium to its underlying assets)

Web address: http://ukpropertyit.invesco.co.uk

Charges: The management team charges 0.85% of gross assets under management.

Income return: Current income is around 6.75 pence per share. When you consider that shares in the fund cost 128 pence each, the income yield is 5.3%.

If you invest in the fund through an ISA that 5.3% income will, of course, be completely tax free. Because most property investors pay income tax on their rental profits that 5.3% is equivalent to earning 8.8% outside an ISA if you're a higher-rate taxpayer.

In other words, if you invest in commercial property outside an ISA you would have to earn an 8.8% rental yield to beat a fund like this which can be held inside an ISA.

It's also critical to point out that 5.3% is net of all costs: interest on borrowings, management fees and so on. The 5.3% is the *net rental profit* paid out to you the investor.

Dividends are paid in February, May August and November.

Remember income from funds such as these is quite predictable and stable. The dividends you receive are simply distributions of rental income and those rents in turn are generated by a large portfolio of quality properties.

Most of the leases in property investment company portfolios have upward-only adjustments so there is strong potential for rents to rise over time.

Capital Growth: The shares have risen from 100p to 128p since the fund was launched in September 2004 – a rise of 28%.

Capital growth is the most uncertain aspect of investing in a property investment company. The property portfolio is revalued every few months to determine the 'net asset value' of the shares.

Of course, during times of rising property prices the valuations will be favourable and the net asset value (NAV) of the shares will increase. That does not, however, mean that the share price will automatically rise. If the share price stays static while the NAV is increasing the fund will start to trade at a discount. Alternatively, the shares may move ahead faster than the growth in the underlying NAV and start trading at a premium.

This is a common experience for investors in closed investment companies such as this.

The worst possible scenario is the share prices start sliding even though the value of the properties remains unchanged. This could happen if there is a loss of confidence in the property sector and investors start bailing out before any major correction in property prices.

The result of this could be the fund moving from a premium to a discount.

Borrowings: The fund has a loan to value ratio of 48%, in other words for every £1 of property assets there is 48p of borrowings.

Geographic allocation: The fund invests in UK property only, primarily in southern England. The portfolio is divided up as follows:

	%
Yorks & Humberside	4.5
West Midlands	13.5
East Midlands	10.5
East	23.4
London	12.9
South East	28.9
South West	6.3

Asset allocation: The managers believe the industrial and office sectors will deliver the strongest performance and provide the highest rental yields so the fund has large holdings in these areas. The portfolio is broken up as follows:

	%
Industrial	46
Offices	40
Retail	8
Other	6

Lease Details

	% of current annual rent
0-3 years	21
3-7 years	18
7-10 years	42
10-15 years	11
15-20 years	3
20+ years	5

Approximately 2.1% of the portfolio by estimated current net annual rent is non income producing.

Invesco UK Property Income Trust
Top 10 Properties

Property Name	£ millions	%
Priory Business Park, Bedford	£23,0	7.7%
Finsgate House, London EC1	£17,9	6.0%
60 Charlotte Street, London W1	£16,9	5.6%
Pegasus Building, Peterborough	£15,3	5.1%
Unit 3, Mercury Drive, Northampton	£13,2	4.4%
Forum 1, Station Road, Theale	£12,0	4.0%
34-62 Staines Road, Hounslow	£11,9	4.0%
Rotherham, Hellaby Lane	£9,5	3.2%
Wootten Bassett, Interface	£9,4	3.1%
Coseley 2, Tipton	£9,3	3.1%

Invesco UK Property Income Trust
Asset Allocation

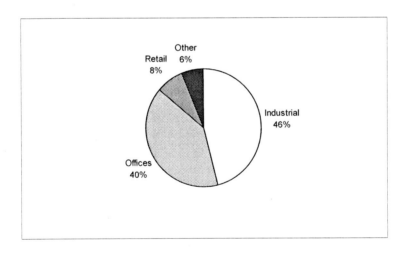

2. ISIS Property Trust Ltd

Introduction

The ISIS Property Trust was launched in October 2003 and has a portfolio of around 35 commercial properties worth £151 million.

The investment objective is to provide an attractive level of income together with income and capital growth. The fund invests in a spread of office, retail and industrial properties.

The fund is structured as a closed-ended Guernsey registered investment company listed on the LSE and Channel Islands Stock exchanges. You'll find the share price online if you go to Yahoo Finance (http://uk.finance.yahoo.com) and type 'IPT' in the share price lookup box.

ISIS is part of F&C Asset Management, one of the UK's leading fund management operations.

Share price: 151p (a 7.4% premium to its underlying assets)

Web address: www.isispropertytrust.co.uk

Income return: Current income is around 7p pence per share. Shares in the fund cost 151p each so the income yield is 4.6%. If you invest in the fund through an ISA that 4.6% is equivalent to earning 7.7% from a direct property held outside an ISA.

The 4.6% income yield is *after all costs*: interest on borrowings, management fees and so on. So it's a *net* income yield.

Dividends are paid in February, May, August and November.

Capital Growth: The ISIS Property Trust has been a good performer in the property company sector. The share price alone has rocketed by around 40% in under two years. And that *excludes* the rental income that is paid out every few months.

Investors have therefore enjoyed a high level of income and capital growth from this fund.

In fact over the last 12 months alone investors have enjoyed a combined return of 26% if you include income and capital growth.

One thing that may put investors off is the fact that the fund is trading at a 7.4% premium. In other words every £1.51 you invest buys you £1.41 of property.

If interest in the fund dries up the premium could turn into a discount and investors would quickly lose money. However, it's worth pointing out that the premium on this fund has been as high as 12%.

Furthermore, every time the portfolio is revalued the net asset value increases, so reducing the premium. The fund's portfolio is revalued every few months and this information is publicised and usually the share price moves accordingly.

Borrowings: The fund has a loan of £48 million. With £151 million of property assets that means the fund has a gearing ratio of 32%.

Geographic allocation: The fund invests in UK property only, primarily in southern England. The portfolio is divided up as follows:

	%
Yorks & Humberside	5.4
West Midlands	2.5
East Midlands	2.4
East	16.9
North East	6.9
South East	37.5
South West	7.7
London West End	7.1
Other London	13.6

Asset allocation: The fund invests in a fairly even spread of shops, offices and industrial properties. The portfolio is broken up as follows:

	%
Industrial	33.5
Offices	30.2
Retail	31.8
Retail warehouse	4.5

Lease Details: The average lease length is 10.6 years and approximately 0.3% of the portfolio is vacant.

ISIS Property Trust Top 10 Properties

Property Name	%
County House, County Square, Chelmsford, Essex	7.3
14, Berkeley Street, London	7.1
18/19, Regent Street, Swindon	7.0
Unit D300 Brooklands,Weybridge, Surrey	5.5
1-2 Network, Eastern Road, Bracknell	5.4
Maxi Centre, Brunel House, Theale	5.2
Units A, B & C, Foundry Lane, Horsham	5.1
Keens House, Anton Mill Road, Andover	5.1
King William House, Market Place, Hull	4.7
111-117, Northumberland Street, Newcastle upon Tyne	4.5
Total	**56.9**

ISIS Property Trust Ltd
Asset Allocation

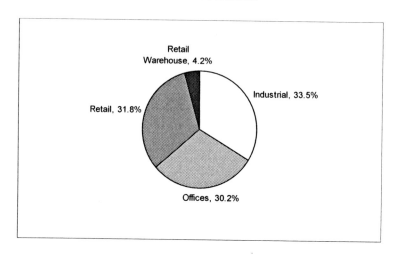

3. ISIS Property Trust 2 Ltd

Introduction
The ISIS Property Trust 2 was launched in June 2004, following the successful launch of the first ISIS Property Trust. The fund has a portfolio of 38 commercial properties worth £209 million.

The investment objective is exactly the same as that of the first ISIS fund: to provide an attractive level of income together with income and capital growth. The fund invests in a spread of office, retail and industrial properties dotted around the UK.

The fund is structured as a closed-ended Guernsey domiciled investment company listed on the London and Channel Islands Stock Exchanges. You'll find the share price online if you go to Yahoo Finance (http://uk.finance.yahoo.com) and type 'IRP' in the share price lookup box.

ISIS is part of F&C group, one of the UK's leading fund management operations.

Share price: 141p (a 10.5% premium to its underlying assets)

Web address: www.isispropertytrust.co.uk

Income return: Current income is around 6.75p pence per share. Shares in the fund cost 141p each so the income yield is 4.8%. If you invest in the fund through an ISA that 4.8% is equivalent to earning 8% from a direct property held outside an ISA.

Once again, the 4.8% income yield is *after all costs*: interest on borrowings, management fees and so on.

Dividends are paid in March, June, September and December.

Capital Growth: Like its sister fund, ISIS Property Trust 2 has delivered attractive returns in recent months. Since its launch the shares have risen by approximately 34%.

Investors have therefore enjoyed a high level of income and capital growth from this fund.

One thing that may also put investors off this ISIS fund is the fact that it is trading at a 10.5% premium. In other words every £1.41 you invest buys you around £1.28 of property.

The fund's portfolio is frequently revalued to determine the value of the property assets. This information is publicised and usually the share price moves accordingly.

Borrowings: The fund has a loan of £70.7 million. With £209 million of property assets that means the fund has a gearing ratio of 34%.

Geographic allocation: The fund invests in UK property only, primarily in southern England. The portfolio is divided up as follows:

	%
Yorks & Humberside	4.1
West Midlands	15.7
East Midlands	2.6
East	2.1
North West	0.7
North East	0.6
South East	49.3
South West	0.7
Central London	14.0
Rest of London	2.1
Scotland	8.1

Asset allocation: The fund has a much larger holding of retail property than, for example, the Invesco fund. The portfolio is broken up as follows:

	%
Industrial	32.2
Offices	23.3
Retail	38.2
Retail warehouse	6.3

Lease Details: The average lease length is 9.9 years and approximately 1.8% of the portfolio (calculated as a percentage of estimated rental values) was vacant at the last reckoning.

ISIS Property Trust 2 Ltd
Top 10 Properties

Property Name	%
Unit 3663, Echo Park, Banbury	7.8
Mercury House, 1 Dove Wynd, Strathclyde Business Park	6.3
48-49, St James's Street, London, SW1	6.3
Southampton International Park, Eastleigh	6.1
Units 1-8, Lakeside Road, Colnbrook	6.0
99/103, Longacre, London, WC2	6.0
30/40, The Parade & 47/59A Warwick Street, Leamington Spa	5.6
Hemel Gateway, Boundary Way, Hemel Hempstead	5.2
Clifton Moor Gate, York	4.1
Swift House, Cosford Lane, Rugby	3.9
Total	**57.3**

ISIS Property Trust 2 Ltd
Asset Allocation

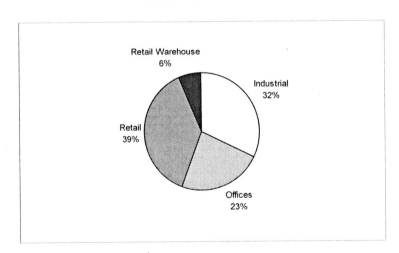

4. Scottish Widows UK Balanced Property Trust

Introduction

The UK Balanced Property Trust was launched in March 2002 and was one of the first property investment funds to set up offshore and target ISA investors.

The fund has properties worth approximately £374 million with a heavy weighting in the retail sector.

The fund is structured as a closed-ended Guernsey domiciled investment company. You'll find the share price online if you go to Yahoo Finance (http://uk.finance.yahoo.com) and type 'UBR' in the share price lookup box.

Based in Edinburgh, Scottish Widows is one of the country's most famous financial institutions. Most of us know them from their TV ads, featuring Amanda Lamb as the young widow, but they're a financial powerhouse with over £80 billion of funds under management.

Share price: 149p (a 6.5% premium to its underlying assets)

Web address: www.swipartnership.com

Income return: Current income is around 7.125p pence per share. Shares in the fund cost 149p each so the income yield is 4.8%. If you invest in the fund through an ISA that 4.8% is equivalent to earning 8% from a direct property held outside an ISA. Once again, that 8% income yield is *net* of all costs.

Dividends are paid in January, April, July and October.

Capital Growth: The fund has performed exceptionally well, delivering a combined return (income and capital growth) of approximately 60% over the last three years.

Borrowings: The fund has a gearing ratio of 31%.

Lease Details: The average lease length is 8.5 years and approximately 2.9% of the portfolio was vacant at the last reckoning.

Scottish Widows UK Balanced Property Trust
Top 10 Properties

Property Name	% Portfolio
The Forum Centre, Sittingbourne	5.0
Radius, Watford	3.5
North Street / Market Street, Guildford	2.9
Brunel Centre, Crawley, RH10 2NT	2.5
The Balmoral Centre, Scarborough	2.5
Units 1-14 Hillmead Complex, Swindon	2.5
Albyn Retail Park, Boston	2.5
Units A-d, Gonerby Road, Grantham	2.3
40 Cumberland Avenue, London	2.3
49-50 High St, Chelmsford	2.6

Scottish Widows UK Balanced Property Trust
Asset Allocation

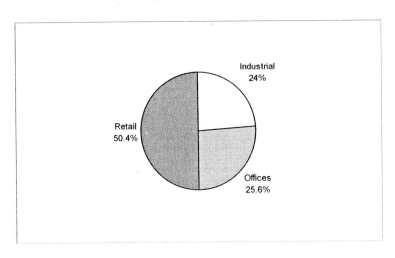

5. Standard Life Property Income Trust

Introduction

The Standard Life Property Income Trust was launched in December 2003 and has a portfolio of 26 properties worth £211 million.

The fund is structured as a closed-ended Guernsey registered investment company. You'll find the share price online if you go to Yahoo Finance (http://uk.finance.yahoo.com) and type 'SLI' in the share price lookup box.

Standard Life is one of the country's biggest fund management groups with assets of over £100 billion under management.

Share price: 138p (a 12.6% premium to its underlying assets)

Web address: http://uk.standardlifeinvestments.com

Income return: The fund aims to pay a dividend of 6.5 pence per share. Shares in the fund cost 138 pence each so the net rental yield is 4.7%. If you invest in the fund through an ISA that 4.7% is equivalent to earning 7.8% from a direct property held outside an ISA. The 4.7% income yield is after all costs: interest on borrowings, management fees and so on.

Dividends are paid in February, May, August and November.

Capital Growth: The Standard Life Property Income Trust has been a good performer since it was launched. In the last year alone it has delivered a total return of 30.3%. Remember this is completely tax free inside an ISA.

Quite a lot of the capital growth since the start of the year has come about thanks to an increase in the fund's premium to net asset value which has risen from a discount of over 2% to a premium of 12.6%.

Borrowings: The fund has a gearing ratio of 43% but aims to increase this to 50% over time.

Lease Details: The average unexpired lease term is 10.2 years.

Standard Life Property Income Trust
Top 10 Properties

Property Name	Location	Value	Type
Clough Road	Hull	£15-£20m	Retail Warehouse
Wellington House	London	£15-£20m	Standard Office
Hollywood Green	London	£15-£20m	Leisure
Drakes Way	Swindon	£5-£10m	Industrial
Wellesley House	Harlow	£5-£10m	Standard Office
Welwyn Garden City	Welwyn	£5-£10m	Office Park
Axys Nantgarw	Cardiff	£5 - £10m	Office Park
White Bear Yard	London	£5 - £10m	Standard Office
Bucknall Street	London	£5 - £10m	Standard Office
Chancellors Place	Essex	£5 - £10m	Standard Office

Standard Life Property Income Trust
Asset Allocation

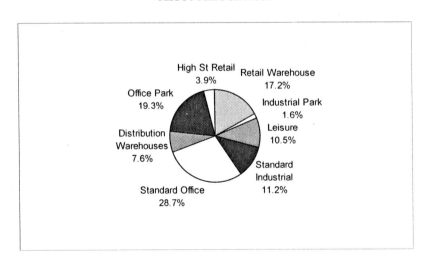

PROPERTY UNIT TRUSTS

1. New Star Property Unit Trust

Introduction
The New Star Property Unit Trust has been around since 1999 and has over £800 million of property assets under management.

New Star is one of the most respected fund management companies in Britain. It was founded by John Duffield, who also founded Jupiter Asset Management.

Like most property funds, the primary aim of New Star's fund is to generate a high income for investors, as well as income growth and capital growth.

The fund's strategy is to invest in commercial property *and* property shares and other securities. So it does not confine its investments to bricks and mortar. About 17% of the portfolio is currently invested in property shares including some big well-known companies such as British Land, Land Securities and Hammerson.

About 67% of the portfolio is invested in around 40 bricks and mortar properties (the top 10 buildings are listed below) and the remaining 16% is invested in deposits and convertibles. Convertibles are investments which earn interest but can be converted into shares at a later date.

The fund invests primarily in the UK but can also invest overseas.

You'll find the latest unit trust price online if you go to Trustnet (www.trustnet.com/ut/funds). Prices are also published daily in the *Financial Times*.

Buying price: 150.97p (income units), 203.69p (accumulation)

Web address: www.newstarinvest.com

Charges: Initial 5%, annual 1.5%.

Minimum investment: £1,000 or £100 per month

Income return: The fund currently has a respectable income yield of 4.1%. Because it's tax free in an ISA, this is equivalent to earning 6.8% from an ordinary rental property.

It's a *net* income yield which means all costs and charges have been deducted so this is the actual cash payout to investors. If you hold accumulation units then this income is automatically reinvested.

Automatic reinvestment of income is something most property investors find almost impossible to do. However, it can have a significant effect on your returns at the end of the day.

Capital Growth: Having been on the scene for several years New Star Property Unit Trust has had time to develop a good track record of generating wealth for investors.

Over the last three years the total return from the fund has been 50%. Again it's important to reiterate that this return would be totally tax free in an ISA.

It's also important to point out – like those annoying ads on TV and radio – that past performance is no guarantee of future performance.

Geographic allocation: The fund invests in UK property only at present, primarily in London and the South East. The portfolio is divided up as follows:

	%
London and South East	87%
North and Midlands	9%
West and South West	3%
East Anglia	1%

The average lease length is 12 years.

Asset allocation

The majority of the fund's bricks and mortar property is invested in offices, followed by industrial property. The fund has very little money invested in the expensive retail sector. The portfolio is broken down as follows:

	%
Industrial	21%
Offices	60%
Retail	17%
Leisure	2%

If you want to get a good feel for the properties in the portfolio go to their online literature library and download the latest interim report for the fund:

www.newstarinvest.com/direct/literature/literature.asp

This document has a lot of information about the individual properties owned by the fund and will give you an interesting insight into how property funds invest your money.

You'll see pictures of properties let out to the likes of Hertz Europe, the Daily Mail, B&Q, Lloyds TSB and other well-known companies.

New Star Property Unit Trust
Top 10 Properties

Property Name	% of Total Fund
Plough Place, Fetter Lane (London EC4)	6.42
Park View, Great West Road (Brentford)	5.66
Royal Mail, Heathrow Gateway	5.25
Ealing Gateway (Ealing)	4.66
Rivers Office Park (Rickmansworth)	4.62
Moorgate, (London EC2)	3.61
1 & 2, Mercury Drive (Northampton)	3.30
EGL, Heathrow Gateway	3.04
Fairmile Place (Cobham)	2.73
Chalfont Grove (Chalfont St Giles)	2.23

New Star Property Unit Trust
Asset Allocation

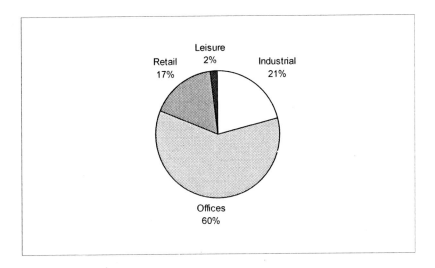

2. Norwich Property Trust

Introduction

Norwich Property Trust is the biggest and oldest property fund you can put in your ISA. It's also widely regarded as the best. In a recent survey of five financial advisers, four chose this fund as one of their favourites.

The fund has been around since 1991 and has performed consistently well. And in an industry dominated by men you may be interested to know that the boss of this fund is a woman. With over £2 billion of property assets to look after every day, Gerardine Davies is arguably the most powerful woman in property in Britain.

Like other property unit trusts the Norwich Property Trust invests mainly in bricks and mortar but also holds some property shares. Approximately 74% of the fund is invested in 109 physical properties, 14% is invested in property shares and 12% is held in cash.

The property shares are split between big companies (the likes of British Land and Liberty International) and small and medium-sized companies (the likes of Great Portland Estates and Brixton).

Buying price: 172.33p (income units), 185.58p (accumulation)

Web address: www.norwichunion.com in 'Money & Investing', 'Norwich Union Unit Trusts'. Or you can call 0845 302 2559.

Charges: Initial 5%, annual 1.42%.

Minimum investment: £1,000 or £30 per month.

Income return: The yield on this fund is extremely low – just 2.6%. In an ISA that's equivalent to earning a net rental yield of 4.3% from a traditional property investment. This is far lower than many of the listed property companies and therefore possibly not ideal for investors searching for high income.

However, what the fund has delivered in buckets in recent years is capital growth.

Capital Growth: In the last year alone the fund has delivered a total return of 16% and in the last three years total returns have been 54% – all tax free in an ISA.

Will these returns continue to be achieved in future? Without a crystal ball there's no way of knowing for certain. However, the experts who run the Norwich fund still believe there is money to be made:

"In terms of the outlook it is undoubtedly true to say that we do not expect returns going forward to be as strong as those which we have seen in the last few years – though it is also fair to say that we have been thinking this for a while now, in common with many property experts, and yet the market is as strong now as it has been.

"It is very likely that this strength will continue in the short term as cashflows show no signs of slowing – very much the reverse. The extension of the ISA regulations, the removal of the option to invest SIPPs in residential property and the introduction of REITs in due course are all likely to support the market, however we do believe that a slowdown will begin in the not-too-distant future.

"We are not, however, forecasting a crash. Our five year forecast for the overall market suggests an average annual return of about 7% which compares with 13.3% per year over the last five years."

Geographic allocation: The fund invests in UK property only and, unlike some of the other funds, has assets spread all over the country. The portfolio is divided up as follows:

	%
London	13.8
South East	24.3
East and south west	17.5
Midlands and Wales	15.2
North and Scotland	29.2

Asset allocation: Just like the geographic spread, the fund's sector spread is also broad.

	%
Industrial	15.8
Offices	33.3
Shops	17.8
Shopping centres	7.8
Retail warehouse	23.7
Other	1.6

Norwich Property Trust
Asset Allocation

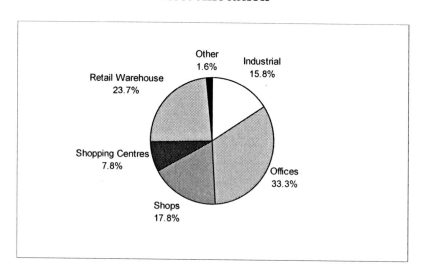

3. M&G Property Portfolio

Introduction

The M&G Property Portfolio was only launched in November 2005 so it doesn't have much of a track record yet. However, it's run by Prudential Property Investment Managers which is one of the largest property investors in the UK with around 1,000 properties worth £15 billion. John Cartwright, the fund's manager has over 30 years experience in commercial property.

Furthermore the fund is already a significant force with around £400 million in assets.

Buying price: 102.9p (income units)

Web address: www.mandg.co.uk

Charges: Initial charge 5%, annual charge, 1.5%

Minimum investment: £1,000, thereafter £100

Income Yield: 3.4%

Geographic allocation

	%
Central London	14
Greater London	8.1
South-East	24.1
South-West	3.8
Rest of UK	50

Asset allocation

	%
Shops	38.9
Retail warehouses	5.2
Offices	33.1
Industrial	21.5
Other	1.3

4. Skandia Property Fund

Introduction
Another new kid on the block, Skandia Property Fund was launched in December 2005 and currently has 23 investments in its £288 million portfolio.

The main aim is to invest in buildings but the portfolio may include property shares, property derivatives and holdings in other property funds.

Its biggest holdings include Currys in Purley Way, Croydon; the Oakhill Industrial Estate in Manchester and a number of buildings in London including 52 Conduit St and 1 Carey Lane.

Buying price: 56.91p (income units), 57.08p (accumulation)

Web: www.skandiainvestmentmanagement.com/funds/

Charges: Initial charge 5%, annual charge, 1.35%

Minimum investment: £1,000, regular savings £50 per month

Income Yield: 4.8%

Geographic allocation

	%
Central London	20.2
Greater London	11.4
South-East	22.2
Rest of UK	46.2

Asset allocation

	%
Retail	40.2
Offices	29.3
Industrial	22.1
Cash	4.1
Equities	3.1

5. Standard Life Select Property Fund

Introduction
Another newbie, this fund was launched in October 2005. The Select Property Fund will offer the benefits of geographically diversified commercial property exposure by investing in a combination of direct property and indirect property vehicles, both listed and unlisted in the UK, Europe, Asia and North America.

The initial portfolio will consist of:

- Direct – UK (Europe within six months of launch): 20-40%
- Unquoted – principally UK-focused property funds: 10-15%
- Quoted – to include UK, Europe, US and Asia: 20-30%
- Corporate bonds and cash – up to 25%

The fund was up 12% in just over 3 months. However, it's important to point out that a lot of the investments are in property shares which may make it more risky.

Web: www.selectpropertyfund.co.uk

Charges: Initial charge 5%, annual charge, 1.75%

Minimum investment: £500, regular savings £50 per month

Income Yield: 3.9%

Asset allocation

	%
Bonds/Cash	6
USA	19
Asia (other)	1
Australia	10
Japan	11
HK/Singapore	10
Europe (ex UK)	16
UK	27

6. Scottish Widows Property Unit Trust

Introduction

Launched in November 2004 this fund now has 67 investments worth £800 million under management. The trust invests mainly in the UK but can also invest in the US and Europe, in property shares and property investment companies, property derivatives, government securities and cash.

The fund has a heavy weighting in retail properties but some of these are being sold and the proceeds invested in offices, especially in central London where rental growth is expected to be strongest.

Investments include the likes of Huddersfield Retail Park which has tenants such as Next and Sportsworld. The top 10 investments are listed below.

The fund has delivered a total return 14% over the last year. However, the fund managers believe the market has peaked and expect gains of around 6-7% per annum over the next five years.

Buying price: 122.58 (income units), 127.38 (accumulation)

Web: www.swipartnership.com

Charges: Initial charge 5%, annual charge, 1.35%

Minimum investment: £5000, regular savings £50 per month

Income Yield: 2.97%

Geographic allocation

	%
London	22.74
South-East	25.41
South-west	6.92
East and West Midlands	4.6
Eastern	10.3
Yorks/Humberside	13.19
North & Scotland	16.84

Scottish Widows Property Unit Trust
Top 10 Properties

Property	% of Portfolio
Great Northern Retail Park, Huddersfield	8.2
Goldstone Retail Park, Hove	6.6
Church Street, Liverpool	4.7
B & Q Store, Cambridge	3.2
66/68 Briggate, Leeds	2.9
17 Dominion Street, London	2.6
Commonwealth Hse Airport, Manchester	2.6
9/11 St Martin's Court, London	2.5
20/24 Queen St, Oxford	2.3
76 King St, Manchester	2.3

Scottish Widows Property Trust
Asset Allocation

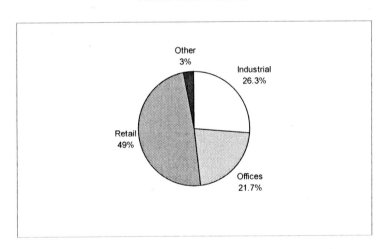

Chapter 7

ISAs vs Pensions

Introduction

Which is a better place to put your money: a property ISA or a property pension?

This is a very important question. ISAs and pensions are the two most important tax shelters available to private investors in the UK.

I've read lots of articles comparing the benefits and drawbacks of each but most never seem to hit the nail on the head.

Despite Gordon Brown's recent u-turn on residential property pensions you can still put commercial property investments in a SIPP, including the property investment funds I listed in the previous chapter.

By investing in property funds through a pension you can:

- Buy at a 40% discount, thanks to the income tax relief on your contributions.

- Avoid paying capital gains tax or income tax on your property profits.

- Potentially reduce the income tax on your entire salary or business profits to zero.

ISA investors don't enjoy any income tax relief so ISAs and pensions have only one major thing in common:

Tax-free investment returns

Both types of investment offer tax-free growth, so no income tax or capital gains tax is payable on your dividends, rental income, interest or capital gains.

The differences are more numerous, as you will see shortly.

As I've said several times in this guide: there is no right way or wrong way to invest, only what works for you. The ISA versus pension decision is not an all-or-nothing one – you can invest in both property ISAs and property pensions.

In this chapter I'm going to outline the various differences between ISAs and pensions so you can decide for yourself which is a better home for your money.

After that, using a detailed example, we'll take a look at the returns each type of investor is likely to enjoy.

Property ISA Benefits

ISAs offer a number of advantages over property pensions:

- **Tax-free income**. ISA investors can withdraw their investment income – dividends, interest and rental income distributions – completely tax free. They can also withdraw their capital gains or their original contributions without paying a penny in tax.

  Pension investors pay income tax on any money withdrawn from their pension plans, be it income, capital gains *or their original contributions*.

- **Flexibility**. ISAs are extremely flexible investments that allow you to access your savings *at any time.*

  Pension savers can only access their money when they reach the minimum retirement age: 50 in the case of personal pensions but usually 60 or 65.

  Even then they cannot get their hands on their savings, only the income.

  This in my opinion is one of the biggest benefits of investing in an ISA rather than a pension plan.

- **Limited Income Choices**. Pension investors usually end up buying an annuity with 75% of their savings (the rest can be taken as a tax-free lump sum).

  This annuity is fully taxed even though some of each payment is simply repayment of your original capital and not investment income.

  From April 2006 there is more flexibility for pension investors. For starters you do not have to buy an annuity and can keep your pension savings invested and withdraw income as and when you please.

  However, there will be restrictions on how much you can withdraw each year.

  Most retirees will probably be compelled by personal circumstances to buy an annuity to maximize their incomes.

- **Age limits**. You cannot keep contributing to a pension indefinitely. Once you reach age 75 you have to stop contributing.

  There is no age restriction for ISA investments and you can withdraw money and make new contributions continually.

- **Earnings requirement**. You can only make big pension contributions if you have 'earnings' – generally a salary or business profits.

  You cannot make significant pension contributions if you are, for example, a non-working spouse, retiree or derive all your income from investments such as property. These groups are limited to an investment of £3,600 per year.

  There is no such restriction on ISA investments. Anyone can invest £7,000 per year.

- **Inheritance planning**. When you die your ISA savings will be paid to your heirs as a lump sum. Pension investors who are already receiving an annuity cannot leave their pension savings to their heirs. The monies will be taken away by the insurance company to subsidize the pensions of others.

If you are not already taking an annuity income, it may be possible in terms of the new pension regulations to leave your savings to close family members in the form of a family pension.

Property Pension Benefits

- **Income-tax relief**. Only pensions provide up-front income tax relief. In other words, if you invest £1,000 you get a refund of the income tax you've paid on £1,000 of your salary or business income.

  Some of this money is paid into your pension plan, the rest is refunded directly. This is a very powerful tax relief which allows you to buy your investments at a 40% discount.

- **Property investment**. ISAs cannot be used to invest *directly* in property. Pensions can currently be used to invest in both property funds and direct commercial property.

- **Investment limits**. The maximum annual ISA investment is £7,000 per person. The maximum pension investment you can make is much higher. From April 6th 2006 you will be able to invest the *lower* of:

  - Your entire annual earnings or
  - £215,000

  For example, if you earn a salary of £60,000 and have made a profit of £60,000 from selling an investment property, you'll be able to invest all that property cash in a pension plan and in the process wipe out your entire income tax bill on your salary for the year!

  This change will make pension plans one of the most powerful tax shelters ever seen.

- **Uncertain future**. The future of ISAs is somewhat uncertain. We know that it will be possible to invest £7,000 per year until 2010. However, the allowance has not been increased to take account of inflation for many years.

After 2010 what will happen to the ISA tax shelter is anyone's guess. It may be scrapped, although this is probably unlikely given the need to encourage personal savings.

Summary

ISAs and pensions have many benefits and drawbacks. The most important benefit of ISAs over pensions is that ISAs allow you to withdraw income tax free. Pension income is fully taxed. ISAs are also extremely flexible investments which allow you to withdraw money at any time.

Pensions offer very generous income tax relief which lets you buy all your investments at a 40% discount and they also allow you to invest directly in property and make large annual contributions.

A very important question is, how do ISAs compare with pensions pound for pound? Which is the more powerful tax planning tool?

In other words, which is more valuable at the end of the day: income tax relief on your original investment (pensions only) or tax-free income when you start making withdrawals (ISAs only)?

To answer this question let's track two investors over time, one investing in a pension the other investing outside a pension.

Example

Peter and Ian, both higher-rate taxpayers, want to invest £3,000 per year each.

Peter uses a personal pension plan. He makes an initial contribution of £3,900 to which the taxman adds a further £1,100 in tax relief. He then claims back £900 when completing his tax return.

All in all Peter has £5,000 of investments which have only cost him £3,000.

(The £1,100 top-up payment is known as basic-rate tax relief. The £900 refund is known as higher-rate relief.)

Ian goes for an ISA and invests £3,000 per year. He doesn't get any tax relief on his contributions so his total investment is just £3,000. (Although the future of the ISA tax break is uncertain I am making the somewhat bold assumption that a tax-free investment allowance of this type will still exist after 2010.)

Both invest in property investment funds and earn 7% per year. These returns are completely tax free for both the ISA investor and the pension investor. They increase their contributions by 3% per year to compensate for inflation.

We track how both investors perform from year to year in Table 2. At the end of year 1 they have £5,350 and £3,210 respectively, which is simply their initial investments of £5,000 and £3,000 plus 7% investment growth.

Peter gets out of the blocks much faster than Ian and after just one year already has £2,140 more than Ian: £2,000 in pension tax relief plus 7% growth on that tax relief.

After five years he has £32,538 compared with Ian's £19,523; after 10 years he has £33,343 more than Ian; after 20 years he has £110,401 more than Ian and after 30 years he has £277,397 more money.

So even though they're both earning an identical tax-free return of 7% and making identical investments, Peter is much better off than Ian. This is because his annual investment is boosted by income tax relief on his contributions.

In fact, Ian always has 60% as much money as Peter. Peter's extra 40% is thanks to the income tax relief he receives on his pension contributions.

Table 2
Pension Returns vs ISA Returns

End Year	Pension	ISA
1	5,350	3,210
2	11,235	6,741
3	17,697	10,618
4	24,782	14,869
5	32,538	19,523
6	41,018	24,611
7	50,278	30,167
8	60,377	36,226
9	71,381	42,828
10	83,358	50,015
11	96,383	57,830
12	110,535	66,321
13	125,900	75,540
14	142,570	85,542
15	160,642	96,385
16	180,222	108,133
17	201,423	120,854
18	224,366	134,619
19	249,179	149,507
20	276,003	165,602
21	304,986	182,991
22	336,287	201,772
23	370,079	222,047
24	406,543	243,926
25	445,876	267,526
26	488,289	292,974
27	534,007	320,404
28	583,272	349,963
29	636,341	381,805
30	693,493	416,096

Income Comparison

Although Ian's total savings are much lower than Peter's, that's not the end of the story.

Firstly, Ian can get his hands on all of his money at any time and do anything he wants with it.

Secondly, Ian can use his ISA savings to pay himself a tax-free income. Peter will have to pay tax at up to 40% on any money he withdraws.

To see what level of after-tax income each investor enjoys, let's assume their money is invested in property investment funds paying income of 5% per year.

Peter will pay 40% tax on this income because it comes out of a pension plan.

So, for example, if he starts withdrawing benefits after 10 years his income will be:
£83,358 x 5% less 40% tax = £2,501

Ian's ISA income will be:
£50,015 x 5% less 0% tax = £2,501

Their after-tax incomes are *identical*! Peter may have received 40% income tax relief on his pension contributions but he also has to pay 40% tax on his income. This puts him back in the same position as Ian the ISA investor.

This is a fascinating result because it shows that the ISA tax shelter is just as powerful as the pension tax shelter.

And the ISA tax shelter comes without the severe restriction imposed on pension savers: ISA savers can get their hands on their money at any time, not just when they retire.

Even this, however, is not necessarily the end of the story.

If Peter pays tax at less than 40% on his pension income he will end up with more money than Ian.

Table 3
Final Income: Pension vs ISA

	Pension taxed @ 40% £	Pension taxed @ 22% £	ISA tax free £
After 5 years	976	1,269	976
After 10 years	2,501	3,251	2,501
After 15 years	4,819	6,265	4,819
After 20 years	8,280	10,764	8,280
After 25 years	13,376	17,389	13,376
After 30 years	20,805	27,046	20,805

This is extremely likely because most people become basic-rate taxpayers when they retire (at present, anyone earning around £37,000 per year or less is a basic-rate taxpayer).

In the example above if Peter pays tax at 22% instead his final income will be:

£83,358 x 5% less 22% tax = £3,251

This time he is earning 30% more income than Ian the ISA investor and is clearly significantly better off.

Table 3 above compares pension and ISA income over different investment periods.

In each case the pension investor is only better off if he ends up paying tax at just 22%.

Finally, I've ignored the fact that pension investors can withdraw 25% of their retirement capital as a tax-free lump sum. After 10 years Peter could therefore sell £20,840 worth of property fund units or shares and withdraw this money from his SIPP.

He could invest the cash in property ISAs over the next few years and earn some tax-free income.

His income will then rise to £3,480 compared with the £2,501 earned by Ian the ISA investor.

In summary, if you withdraw a tax-free lump sum from your pension and are a basic-rate taxpayer when you retire, you could be better off with a SIPP rather than an ISA.

Note that withdrawing 25% of your pension capital is not an option open to SIPP investors who have traditional bricks and mortar property investments. Why? Because this would mean selling an entire property which may not be desirable if the property is an attractive income producer.

Summary

- Pensions and ISAs have one major thing in common: there is no tax on investment returns, including interest, dividends, rental income distributions and capital gains.

- ISAs are much more flexible than pensions. You can withdraw money at any time. Pension investors have to wait until they reach the minimum retirement age.

- ISA investors pay no tax on any income they withdraw. Pension withdrawals are fully taxed.

- Pensions provide a number of benefits not available to ISA investors: income tax relief on contributions, the opportunity to make large lump sum investments and the opportunity to invest directly in property.

- The pension benefit of upfront income tax relief is worth the same as the ISA benefit of tax-free income. The only way a pension investor will end up with more money is if he or she only pays 22% tax or withdraws a tax-free lump sum and invests it in an ISA.

Chapter 8

ISAs vs Paying Off Your Mortgage

Most of us know that small increases in monthly house payments can knock years off the life of a mortgage. There is nothing magical about this. Every extra £1 you pay off, is a £1 on which you do not have to pay interest over many years.

To illustrate this effect, Table 4 shows how increasing monthly payments by between 5% and 20% will shorten the life of a typical mortgage. The numbers in the table show what percentage of the total debt remains unpaid at different points in time.

For example, if you increase your mortgage payments by 10% then after 10 years you will have 53% of your debt left. If you have made no increase in your payments you will still have 65% left to pay off.

The attraction of using that extra £1 to pay off your mortgage, as opposed to investing it elsewhere, is down to the taxman's unequal treatment of the interest you earn versus the interest you pay:

Interest earned is usually taxed, interest paid is not tax deductible.

Higher-rate taxpayers who earn 5% on their savings are left with only 3% after the taxman has taken his slice. This means they earn just £3 per year on every £100 of savings.

What about the interest they pay? If the mortgage interest rate is 6%, they will pay £6 per year on every £100 of debt.

Effectively you pay twice as much interest as you earn on identical sums of money.

Table 4
Mortgage Outstanding

End of year	Extra Mortgage Payments			
	0%	5%	10%	20%
1	97	97	96	96
2	94	94	93	91
3	91	90	89	86
4	88	86	84	81
5	85	82	80	75
6	81	78	75	69
7	77	74	70	63
8	73	69	65	56
9	69	64	59	49
10	65	59	53	41
11	60	53	46	33
12	55	47	39	24
13	49	41	32	15
14	43	34	24	6
15	37	27	16	Paid off
16	31	19	8	
17	24	11	Paid off	
18	16	2		
19	8	Paid off		
20	Paid off			

One way to beat the tax system and your bank manager is to use your savings to pay off your mortgage early. This strategy is based on the following principle:

Not having to pay interest is better than earning it.

If your mortgage interest rate is 6 per cent, by not having to pay that 6 per cent on the extra house payments you make, you have effectively earned an after-tax return of 6 per cent.

The interest payments you have saved are equivalent to earning a savings rate of 10% (10% less 40% tax leaves you with 6%).

There isn't a savings product alive that offers such high and secure returns!

There are also non-tax reasons for making extra mortgage payments. Firstly, with the launch of so many 'flexible mortgages', the extra money you pay in does not necessarily disappear out of reach. If you require the cash for some other purpose you should be able to extract it easily.

Secondly, the fact that lending rates are usually much higher than savings rates is another reason why not having to pay interest is more attractive than earning it.

In summary, it is almost always better to pay off your mortgage than invest in a regular *taxed* savings account.

But what about tax-free savings accounts like ISAs – is it better to invest in them or concentrate on paying off your mortgage? The examples that follow will hopefully help you answer this important question.

Example

Ricky and Caroline have a 20 year mortgage of £250,000. At the present interest rate of 6 per cent their monthly repayment is £1,791.

They're now trying to decide whether to increase their mortgage payment by 20% (£358 per month) or put the money in a low-risk cash ISA or bond ISA, earning 6% per year.

If they invest in an ISA they will simply put away an extra £358 per month for 20 years and carry on paying off their mortgage as normal.

Alternatively, if they increase their monthly mortgage repayments by £358, their debt will be liquidated after 14 years and 6 months.

They can then spend the final five and a half years saving aggressively. At that point they will be able to invest both the £1,791 that would have been paid into their mortgage account *and* they can invest the additional £358 per month.

Which strategy is best?

In each case total monthly payments of £2,149 (£1,791 plus £358) are made into the ISA, mortgage account or a combination of both.

As it happens, both strategies produce *identical* returns: After 20 years Ricky and Caroline will end up with a house that is fully paid off and £166,000 of tax sheltered ISA savings.

However, there's one fatal error in the above example: I assumed that the interest rate on the ISA is the same as the interest rate on the mortgage. In practice, savings rates are rarely if ever as high as borrowing rates and you could expect the ISA rate to be at least 1% lower than the mortgage rate.

Changing interest rates has a significant effect on the outcome, as the following example illustrates.

Example revisited

Returning to Ricky and Caroline, let's assume they earn 5% on their ISA savings and pay 6% on their mortgage. If this is the case then concentrating on paying off the mortgage (which has the higher interest rate) is probably the best strategy.

After 20 years Ricky and Caroline will end up with a fully paid house and ISA savings of about £162,000. The ISA savings, remember, are built up after the mortgage has been fully repaid.

If instead they had made monthly ISA investments from the very beginning they would eventually end up with a house and just £147,000 of savings.

In conclusion, paying off a mortgage is possibly more attractive than investing in cash ISAs. Not having to pay 6% is better than earning 5%.

This is still not necessarily the end of the story. ISA investment may be more attractive than repaying a mortgage in certain circumstances, as we shall now see.

Why ISAs Might Still be Best

In the above example Ricky and Caroline could choose between investing their £358 monthly savings in a cash ISA or paying off their mortgage.

In reality, they have lots of other investments to choose from. In particular they could put their money in a property ISA or a FTSE tracker ISA and there's little doubt that, over a long period of time such as 20 years, they'll earn much more than from a cash ISA.

Example revisited... again

Let's assume Ricky and Caroline earn 7% per year from a property ISA for 20 years (hardly an outlandish assumption) and still pay 6% on their mortgage.

If this is the case then using their surplus £358 to accumulate ISA savings is preferable to paying off the mortgage. Why? For the simple reason that the property ISA delivers a return higher than the mortgage interest rate.

If Ricky and Caroline pay off their mortgage as normal and invest their extra £358 per month in a property fund from day one, after 20 years they will end up with a fully paid house and ISA savings of about £188,000.

If instead they pay the extra money into their mortgage, repay the house six years early and only then invest in a property ISA, they will end up with a house and just £172,000 of savings.

Let's be a bit cocky now and assume that Ricky and Caroline earn 10% per year from their property ISA. In these circumstances, investing surplus savings in an ISA from day one will leave them with investments worth £274,000. If instead they pay off the house early and only then start investing in a property ISA they will end up with just £188,000 of investments.

In conclusion, paying off a mortgage is NOT attractive if you think you can earn more than the mortgage interest rate over a long period of time.

However, it's always worth remembering that investing in shares or property investment funds is a lot more risky than paying off your debts.

After all you have no way of knowing what sort of return you will achieve.

Chapter 9

The Best Self-select ISAs and ISA Supermarkets

If you want to invest in a property investment company you have to open what's known as a self-select ISA. If you want to invest in a property unit trust you can either contact the fund management company directly or buy through an ISA supermarket.

Self-select ISAs

If you want to invest in one of the property investment companies discussed in Chapter 6, do not contact the likes of Standard Life or Scottish Widows directly. These funds are not investment products as such – they're listed companies whose shares are purchased through stockbrokers and the like using a self-select ISA.

These are to ISAs what SIPPs are to pensions. In other words, they offer complete flexibility, allowing you to buy and sell any shares that take your fancy.

Some self-select ISAs also let you invest in unit trusts.

Self-select ISAs usually let you switch easily from one investment to another, paying just dealing costs for individual shares and low initial charges on investment funds.

Anyone who wants to take complete control of their investments should consider a self-select ISA.

You can also keep your money in cash, pending investment, if you're nervous about making property or stock market investments straight away.

You cannot open a joint ISA with your spouse but there's nothing to stop each of you from opening one.

Self-select ISAs are available from many stockbrokers, including online stockbrokers and certain high street banks and other financial companies:

- Halifax - www.halifax.co.uk/sharedealing

- Barclays - www.stockbrokers.barclays.co.uk

- Killik & Co - www.killikisa.co.uk

- Hargreaves Lansdown - www.hargreaveslansdown.co.uk

- Squaregain (formerly Comdirect) - www.squaregain.co.uk

- Alliance Trusts – www.alliancetrusts.com

Halifax was voted the best stockbroker in 2003 and 2004 by *What Investment* magazine. Squaregain won the sharedealing category in the Consumer Finance Awards 2004. Alliance Trusts won the Best Stocks & Shares ISA category in the 2003 Consumer Finance Awards.

Self-select ISAs are usually more expensive than ordinary ISAs but they've become extremely competitive in recent years and there are some great deals available from some of the online brokers.

When choosing a self-select ISA there are a number of factors to consider:

- **The cost per trade.** These charges have fallen dramatically in recent years. For example, Halifax charges just £11.95 per trade. Some brokers charge less if you make a large number of trades. For example, Barclays charges just £7.50 per trade after you've completed 10 trades in a three month period.

- **Annual Admin charge.** Some brokers such as Alliance Trusts do not levy any annual fee. Others such as Squaregain charge a flat fee of £25 per year and others such as Halifax and Barclays charge a percentage, typically around 0.5% per year with a maximum of, say, £80 per year.

- **Investment choice.** Some self-select ISAs offer a bigger range of shares and investment funds than others. For example, some offer foreign stocks, others don't. If you're interested in investing in property investment company shares or property unit trusts I suggest you check that they are on your chosen broker's menu.

  Alliance Trusts is one of the only self-select ISA providers that provides a comprehensive list of every share and fund that you can invest in. Most of the property investment company shares appear on that list but not many property unit trusts.

- **Exit penalties.** If you wish to switch to a new ISA there may be an exit charge. It's advisable to check up on this *before* you open a self-select ISA. It's only after you open an account that you will discover what quality of service is provided so it is advisable to keep your options open.

ISA Supermarkets

If you want to invest in a property unit trust ISA you can either invest directly through the fund manager (using, for example, the contact details provided in Chapter 6), get in contact with a good IFA or invest through an ISA supermarket.

ISA supermarkets allow you to choose from a broad range of investment funds and switch from one to another at low cost. They're an excellent idea because you may decide after a couple of years to switch into a more exciting fund offered by a different company.

Some of the best-known supermarkets include:

- Fidelity's FundsNetwork:
  www.fidelity.co.uk/direct/select/fundsnetwork

- Fundsdirect:
  www.fundsdirect.co.uk

- Cofunds:
  www.cofunds.co.uk

Most supermarkets do not offer every property unit trust but most have a selection. At the time of writing Cofunds seemed to offer one of the biggest selections:

www.cofunds.co.uk/docs/FundsAvailable.pdf

Another benefit of investing through an ISA supermarket is that many have negotiated attractive discounts with the fund providers.

For example, if you use Fundsdirect to invest in the New Star or Norwich property unit trusts the upfront charges are just 3% and 2.25% respectively, compared with 5% if you invest directly.

Chapter 10

How to Save £7,040 Extra in Tax Every Year

Every person enjoys an annual capital gains tax exemption which means you can make tax-free profits of £8,800 during the tax year starting on April 6th 2006. Married couples can make profits of £17,600.

This means you can save up to £7,040 in tax (£17,600 x 40%) by making full use of your CGT exemptions this year.

To do this, however, you have to *sell* assets and crystallise a profit.

This may not suit all investors, especially those who want to hold their property funds or other assets as long-term investments.

A few years ago it was possible to sell your shares or unit trusts and buy them back the next day. This was called 'bed and breakfasting'. If you do this now you'll fall foul of the taxman's anti-avoidance rules.

These rules makes it difficult to buy back shares at any time within 30 days of selling them.

However, there are ways of getting around the anti-avoidance legislation. One way is to get your spouse to buy the assets back (see Carl Bayley's guide *Tax Planning for Couples* for a detailed explanation).

Bed & ISA

Another way of avoiding the anti-avoidance rules is to sell your shares and *repurchase them through an ISA*. The ISA is regarded as the new legal owner in the eyes of the taxman and therefore you have not legally bought back the investments.

Example

Aru and his wife Karthika have some shares in Big Bucks plc. They originally paid £1,000 for the shares which have now increased in value to £14,000.

They haven't used their annual CGT exemptions yet so they decide to sell the shares and realise some tax-free profits.

The profit of £13,000 is easily covered by their combined annual exemptions and is therefore totally tax free.

They're both extremely excited about the company's long-term prospects and want to buy the shares back immediately.

They cannot do this directly as they will fall foul of the taxman's anti-avoidance rules. Waiting 30 days before repurchasing the shares is also not acceptable as they expect them to keep rising in the short term.

So they decide to buy them back though a maxi ISA. Fortunately their total investment is worth exactly £14,000 – the maximum ISA investment for a couple!

Any future profits will then, of course, be sheltered from tax permanently.

Other Issues

When adopting this strategy there are some other important issues to keep in mind:

- **Stamp duty.** When you buy shares you have to pay stamp duty. Fortunately at 0.5% the rate is quite low.

- **Other trading costs**. You also have to pay dealing costs and will be hit by the buy/sell spread on the shares (the difference between the bid price and the offer price).

- **Unit trusts upfront charges.** Share trading costs are usually quite low and so you would probably have little to lose by selling your shares to take advantage of your annual

CGT exemption. With unit trusts it's a different story – upfront costs can be as high as 5%. So when you repurchase your units through an ISA you may have to pay these costs a second time.

Example

Jonathan bought £3,000 worth of units in a property unit trust five years ago. They've now risen in value to £6,000. He decides to sell them to make use of his CGT exemption. Doing so will potentially save him £1,200 in tax (£3,000 profit x 40% tax).

However, when he rebuys the units he may have to pay an upfront charge of 5% or more. On a £6,000 investment this charge will come to £300, eating up quite a lot of his potential tax savings.

- **Big Investors**. It's also important to remember that ISA investments are limited to just £7,000 per person per year so selling shares and reinvesting in an ISA is not suitable for very big investors with large gains on their hands.

- **Using Your Spouse**. One alternative to Bed & ISA is 'Bed & Spouse'. In terms of this strategy one spouse sells the shares and the other buys them back immediately.

Summary

If you already own shares or unit trusts that have made significant profits the Bed & ISA strategy is a useful way of realising some profits tax free and getting around the taxman's anti-avoidance rules.

Chapter 11

Making the Most of Cash ISAs

The great thing about cash ISAs is that, not only are the returns tax free, but the banks and building societies usually offer much higher interest rates on ISAs than on regular savings accounts.

Make sure you're earning *at least* the Bank of England base rate and preferably a bit more than that (the base rate can easily be found at www.bankofengland.co.uk).

Some banks offer a slightly higher rate if you're prepared to provide notice of, say, 30 days rather than have instant access to your cash.

Others also offer high fixed rates if you're prepared to tie your money up for several years.

Most banks will also offer you a higher return if you have a large lump sum to invest, for example, if you're transferring over £10,000 of existing ISA savings. Never be shy to ask a bank for a higher rate if you think you have the financial muscle to back it up. Like most things in life, interest rates are often negotiable.

How do ISA cash returns compare with taxed savings accounts? If you're a higher-rate taxpayer, a rate of 5% tax free is equivalent to earning a whopping 8.33% from a regular taxed account. (To get this number simply divide 5 by 0.6 or 60%, which is what you're left with after paying 40% tax.)

There are very few investments which can boast such a high and very safe before-tax return. So the conclusion has to be that cash ISAs are an excellent investment medium for investors who are currently scared of the stock market (and maybe even the property market) and want somewhere safe to store their money.

Cash ISAs have certainly proved popular in recent years with many investors fleeing out of shares and unit trusts. Many property investors are feeling just as cautious at present so cash ISAs are likely to continue to be a popular choice.

There are, of course, other options available to conservative investors, such as gilts and bond funds.

Although the best cash ISAs, paying around 5% at the time of writing, are at first glance appealing, you should never forget that, taxed or untaxed, a bank account is the worst place to store your money *long term*.

With inflation running at around 2.5% the *real* interest rate (roughly speaking the interest rate you earn minus the inflation rate) is only about 2.5%.

In other words, your money may be growing by 5% per year but its real purchasing power is only growing by a puny 2.5% per year.

Investing in a cash ISA is a bit like a woman falling for a man with barn-door shoulders only to find that his impressive physique is thanks to a padded jacket. Cash ISAs are, at best, short-term investments. Don't expect them to make a significant difference to your wealth.

Example

Mr and Mrs Robinson invest a total of £6,000 per year in a cash ISA and earn 5% interest tax free. Both normally pay 40% tax on their non-ISA interest.

After five years they'll have accumulated a nice little nest egg worth £34,811.

How much would their savings be worth if they had simply put their money in an ordinary taxed savings account? In this case, they would end up with £32,810, which means using the ISA tax shelter has earned them an extra £2,000 approximately.

Although they're much better off investing in an ISA, it's still debatable whether they should be keeping their savings in the bank... ISA or no ISA.

Their wealth simply hasn't increased much in *real, inflation-adjusted terms*. To simply beat inflation the Robinson's require £32,326 after five years. That's assuming inflation stays at 2.5% per year.

As we know, they actually ended up with £34,811 which means their wealth has increased by only £2,485 in real terms. No investor should be happy with such a mediocre outcome.

In conclusion, cash ISAs are much better than ordinary bank accounts but it's unlikely you'll see your wealth increase much after adjusting for inflation.

Tax-free Income Again

Where cash ISAs – just like other ISAs – look their best is when used to generate tax-free income.

Example Revisited

As we already know, after five years Mr and Mrs Robinson end up with £32,810 if they invest outside an ISA and £34,811 if they use an ISA. Using an ISA leaves them with just 6% more money.

If they now close their account and use the money to buy things (be it new cars, education for children, a deposit on a property) they will be throwing away a valuable tax break. Far better to keep this money where it is and eventually use it to generate permanently tax-free income.

Using an ISA their £34,811 in savings would produce tax-free income of £1,741 every year.

Without an ISA they would have savings of £32,810 which would produce an after-tax income of just £984.

Although investing in an ISA doesn't leave the Robinsons with much more investment capital, because these savings are permanently sheltered from tax, the after-tax income they produce is 77% higher!

Summary

- Cash ISAs are an attractive short-term investment – the interest rates are competitive and the returns are completely tax free.

- Shop around for the best deal and remember that a higher interest rate is often available if you're happy to tie your savings up for a while or have a large lump sum to invest.

- Although it's far better to put your cash savings inside an ISA your returns will still not be all that great when adjusted for inflation.

Chapter 12

Are Children's ISAs a Good Idea?

Children have their own income tax personal allowances which means they can earn £5,035 per year tax free during the 2006-07 tax year. Thanks to this allowance, a child who does no paid work would need to have close to £100,000 in savings before paying a penny in income tax!

So you could argue that only very rich kids need ISAs. Alternatively, if children earn income from part-time jobs, they may well use up their income tax personal allowances and therefore need to shelter their savings from the taxman.

Even if children are not working, there are three reasons why opening ISAs for them is better than putting money into an ordinary savings account:

- The interest rates are often more attractive than from other savings accounts.
- You have very little to lose. It doesn't cost anything to set up an ISA and there are no penalties if you withdraw funds or close down your account.
- Most important, the ISA could come in handy further down the road when the child becomes an adult taxpayer.

Example

From the age of 16 Damian's wealthy uncle Rodney gives him £3,000 to invest in a cash ISA. Damian finishes school and then goes off to university and only starts working when he's 23. So although he's had ISA savings for eight years he hasn't saved one penny in tax because he isn't a taxpayer yet.

However, when Damian starts working the ISA will start providing a concrete tax benefit. By then he'll have about £28,600 saved and will be earning about £1,400 per year in interest. Because his money has been sheltered in an ISA from day one, the interest is completely tax free.

If the money had been put in a regular savings account instead, Damian's tax bill could be as much as 40% – a whopping £572.

So if you want to give money to children to save for the long-term, an ISA could be extremely useful.

You may notice in the previous example I used Damian's uncle Rodney. If instead the money was given by his father, Derek, this would cause problems.

If parents gives money to their children they have to watch out for the '£100 rule' – if the income exceeds £100 it counts as belonging to the parent for tax purposes. This rule does not apply to grandparents, other relatives or friends.

Adult Children

The above rule applies to minor children. There's nothing to stop you gifting cash to your adult children so that they can have their own ISAs. All income and capital gains will be completely tax free.

Furthermore, the first £3,000 of donations per person per tax year is completely exempt from inheritance tax.

How much tax are gifts such as these likely to save?

Example

Homer and Marge, both higher-rate taxpayers and both making full use of their annual ISA allowances, decide to give their two adult children, Bart and Lisa, £3,000 each per year. Homer and Marge don't have to worry about inheritance tax because the first £3,000 of gifts is exempt.

How much tax will they save over a three-year period? Bart and Lisa invest the money in a cash ISA earning 5%. In total they will earn £4,811 interest over the period. Because it's in an ISA there is no tax to pay.

If Homer and Marge had earned this interest the tax bill would have been £1,924.

Child Trust Funds

While we're on the subject of saving money for children, remember that if your children are born on or after September 1st 2002 they could be eligible for a tax-free Child Trust Fund (CTF).

Parents don't need to claim anything – if child benefit has been paid a voucher for £250 will be sent out in the post along with an information pack.

A range of CTF accounts is available. All providers are making available 'stakeholder' accounts on which charges are low and investment in growth assets such as shares can be made.

The money can only be extracted when the child is 18 years of age and can be used for absolutely any purpose.

Most important of all, parents and other family members and friends can contribute up to £1,200 per year to the CTF account and all returns, as with ISAs, are completely tax free.

For more information go to: www.childtrustfund.gov.uk

Summary

- If you can afford to open an ISA for a child there may not be much tax saved in the short run but the benefit will be felt when the child becomes an adult taxpayer.

- Parents of minor children have to be careful of putting too much money in their names. If income exceeds £250 the whole lot will be taxed in the parents' hands.

- Parents of adult children can donate £3,000 per year without worrying about the inheritance tax consequences and that money can be invested tax free in an ISA.

- Child Trust Funds allow parents of children born since September 2002 to invest £1,200 per year for up to 18 years in a tax-free account.

Answers to Key ISA Questions

In this section I'm going to briefly outline the main ISA rules and answer some of the more frequently asked questions.

To be frank, this is not the most exciting information, which explains why it's put at the back of the book!

However, I encourage you to read it so that you're familiar with the relevant ISA terms and rules.

The real 'meat' is contained in the previous chapters where ISAs are placed under the microscope. These explain how to maximize your ISA tax savings and compare them with other investment products that are competing for your precious savings. Most important of all, I examine how you can use them to make tax-free property investments.

What are the tax benefits of ISAs?

ISA investors don't have to pay any income tax on their interest and dividends or rental income distributions and they don't have to pay any capital gains tax when they sell their shares, bonds, unit trusts or property holdings.

The fact that all returns are tax free is common knowledge. But what is not so widely known is that you have to be very careful *how* you use your ISA allowance if you are going to maximize your tax savings or, indeed, enjoy any tax savings at all.

For example, should you use your ISA allowance to save for a child's education or to supplement your retirement income? Should you use your ISA allowance to invest in shares, bonds or property? These important questions are answered in Chapter 2.

You must also be confident that an ISA is the best investment for YOU. The fact that ISAs are terrific tax shelters does not automatically mean that we should all go out and buy one.

Important questions you should ask yourself include:

- Would I be better off investing in buy-to-let property?

- Would I be better off putting my savings in a pension plan?

- Would I be better off paying off some of my mortgage?

These questions are answered in Chapters 3, 7 and 8 respectively.

In summary, the ISA tax break is extremely valuable but only if you use your savings for the correct purpose and only if you have fully explored your other investment choices.

Do ISAs offer any non-tax benefits?

ISA are primarily a tax-saving device. However, they offer some interesting additional benefits:

- If you're a cash investor, ISA interest rates are often higher than those on regular savings accounts.

- If you're a stock market investor and regularly buy and sell shares the capital gains tax calculations can become extremely time consuming. ISA investors have no calculations to worry about.

- You do not have to declare your ISAs on your tax return. So if privacy is important, an ISA could be ideal.

What's the maximum I can invest?

Most investors know the answer to this question. Every person can invest up to £7,000 per tax year in a 'stocks and shares' ISA.

The tax year starts on April 6th each year and ends on April 5th the following year. So you could, for example, invest £7,000 on April 5th in one year and a further £7,000 the next day.

Alternatively, you could make regular investments of around £580 per month.

Because every *person* is entitled to an ISA allowance, a couple can save up to £14,000 per tax year. If their investments grow by just 7% per year, after five years they will have permanently sheltered not just their £70,000 in contributions but almost £12,000 in tax-free growth.

Because there is no tax on asset transfers between *married* couples, a working spouse can transfer £7,000 to a non-working spouse so that full use can be made of his or her allowance.

Looking ahead, there is some uncertainty as to what a future Government will do with the ISA tax shelter. The allowance was supposed to fall from £7,000 to £5,000 but in the 2005 Budget an announcement was made that the £7,000 limit will be retained until April 5th 2010.

Investors will be able to make investments as follows over the next few years:

Tax year ended April 5th 2006	£7,000
Tax year ended April 5th 2007	£7,000
Tax year ended April 5th 2008	£7,000
Tax year ended April 5th 2009	£7,000
Tax year ended April 5th 2010	£7,000

This means single taxpayers will be able to shelter £35,000 over the next five years and couples will be able to put away as much as £70,000.

How much can I invest in a cash ISA?

The £7,000 limit applies to 'stocks and shares' ISAs. So if you want to put some money into shares, unit trusts, investment trusts, corporate bonds, gilts or property funds you'll be able to invest the full £7,000.

But if you want to put your money in the bank, where it's ultra safe, the maximum investment is just £3,000 per person. This, of course, means that a couple can shelter up to £6,000 per year from tax – which will grow to about £33,500 over a five year period if you include tax-free interest at 5%.

Chapter 11 takes a closer look at how you can make the most of cash ISAs and how to find the very best interest rates available.

What are 'maxi' and 'mini' ISAs?

Instead of simply allowing investments of £7,000 per year in any type of asset, the taxman decided to make our lives a bit more complicated by introducing 'maxi' and 'mini' ISAs.

A maxi ISA can include both cash and stocks and shares. You can only open one maxi ISA in any one tax year.

The total amount you can invest is £7,000. You can invest up to £3,000 of this in the cash element.

Alternatively, you can take out up to two mini ISAs in a single tax year using two different managers. You are allowed up to £4,000 in a stocks and shares ISA and £3,000 in a cash ISA.

You can only open one mini cash ISA and one mini stocks and shares ISA per year.

You cannot take out a maxi and mini ISA in the same tax year.

The most important facts to remember are the following:

- Always make sure you have a maxi ISA if you want to invest more than £4,000 in shares or unit trusts.

- Consider a mini ISA if you want to invest in shares *and* cash. Because you can use a different investment company or bank for each mini ISA, this will allow you to shop around for the highest interest rates.

What is a self-select ISA?

Self-select ISAs are for investors who want complete control over how their money is invested. For example, if you want to choose what shares to buy, rather than rely on a City fund manager, a self-select ISA is the way to go.

Self-select ISAs are offered by numerous stockbrokers and are great for share traders because they can use them to buy and sell shares as often as they like without ever having to worry about capital gains tax (or income tax, for that matter).

Share traders who use ISAs also don't have to worry about the potentially complex capital gains tax calculations that have to be performed before submitting their annual tax returns. This is because your ISA dealings do not have to be declared on your tax return.

Self-select ISAs are also used by investors who want to put their savings into property.

Chapter 9 takes a look at how you should choose a self-select ISA and the various offerings.

What is an ISA supermarket?

If you want to invest in unit trusts and investment trusts, rather than directly in stocks and shares, an ISA supermarket is probably the way to go.

Just like a visit to your local Tesco, ISA supermarkets offer you a wide choice of *products* (you can invest in something exotic like an Asian small company fund, or something conservative like a UK bond fund) and a wide choice of *brand names* (they often have funds from over 50 different investment companies).

You can switch from one type of fund to another and the charges for doing this are usually extremely low or zero.

Who can invest in ISAs?

There aren't many restrictions. First of all you have to be resident and ordinarily resident in the UK for tax purposes (Most people reading this guide will meet this requirement but for a detailed explanation of residence see the Taxcafe guide *Non Resident & Offshore Tax Planning*).

The only other important restriction is your age:

- If you are aged 15 or under, you cannot have any ISA.
- If you are aged 16 or 17, you can have a cash ISA and save up to £3,000 per year tax free. This can be either a mini cash ISA or a maxi ISA where you can only put money into the cash component.
- If you are 18 or over you can invest in any type of ISA. There is no maximum age so you can invest in ISAs even if you are retired and withdrawing a pension.

What assets can I hold in my ISA?

The following investments currently qualify for the £7,000 'stocks and shares' allowance:

- Shares of companies listed on a 'recognised stock exchange', anywhere in the world.
- Corporate bonds of companies listed on recognised stock exchanges, anywhere in the world.
- Gilt-edged securities (gilts) and similar securities issued by other governments in the European Economic Area.
- UK authorised unit trusts or open ended investment companies (OEICs).
- Investment trusts.

In case you're wondering, most stock exchanges are 'recognised' by the Inland Revenue. Visit this web page for a complete list:

www.inlandrevenue.gov.uk/fid/rse.htm

The following investments can be included in a cash ISA:

- Bank and building society cash ISA accounts.
- Money market unit trusts and OEICs.
- National Savings and Investments products which are specially designed for ISAs (but not other National Savings and Investments products such as Savings Certificates or Pensioners' Guaranteed Income Bonds)

What assets can I not hold in an ISA wrapper?

Shares of companies listed on the Alternative Investment Market (AIM), options, futures, and warrants and shares in unquoted companies are excluded.

AIM shares do enjoy periods of spectacular growth and there are fantastic pickings in this sector. Although these stocks cannot be sheltered in an ISA, it's worth pointing out that AIM shares do enjoy their own special tax treatment.

They generally qualify for what's known as 'business asset taper relief' which means that once you've held your shares for more than two years only 25% of your profits are taxed. Effectively this means an AIM investor who holds onto his shares for more than two years will never pay more than 10% tax (40% of 25% = 10%).

Options are popular with experienced investors who wish to 'leverage' or 'gear up' their returns. Options allow you to enjoy exposure to a large amount of shares for a fraction of the cost. Profits are generally subject to capital gains tax.

Option investors therefore face a potential dilemma: invest in shares which deliver lower returns but are potentially tax free through a self-select ISA, or invest in options which offer higher pre-tax returns but 40% of your profits could end up in the taxman's coffers.

What are the CAT standards?

More horrible jargon, I'm afraid. The Government has laid down a set of standards to help you find an ISA that offers reasonable Charges, Access, and Terms (CAT).

Most ISA providers state clearly whether their ISA complies or not and there are different standards for different types of ISA.

For cash ISAs:

- There must be no one-off or regular charges of any kind, such as charges for withdrawals.
- The minimum transaction must be no greater than £10.

- It must be possible to withdraw your money within seven working days or less.
- The interest rate must be no lower than two percentage points below the Bank of England base rate. The base rate can easily be found at www.bankofengland.co.uk.
- If the base rate goes up the ISA rate must follow within one month. Downward changes may be slower.
- There must be no other conditions, such as limits on frequency of withdrawals.

For stocks and share ISAs:

- The annual charge must be no more than 1% of net asset value.
- There must be no other charges such as initial charges.
- You must be able to put in amounts as small as £500 for a lump sum or £50 a month for regular savings.
- Investment may be in authorised unit and investment trusts or in open-ended investment companies (OEICs).
- A fund must be at least 50% invested in ISA-qualifying shares and securities that are listed on European Union stock exchanges.
- Units and shares must be single priced (that is, no separate buying and selling prices).
- Product literature must highlight the investment risk.

Can I transfer to another ISA?

There's a good chance you will at some point want to transfer your existing ISA savings to a new ISA provider. It may be that your existing cash ISA is offering an uncompetitive interest rate or your existing unit trust manager is not performing as well as the competition.

You can transfer your ISA to another ISA manager whenever you want.

You can usually do this by asking the new manager to make the necessary arrangements (make sure the manager you are switching to will accept transfers and ask them for a transfer form).

Your existing ISA manager cannot stop you transferring, but watch out for hidden charges and be prepared to wait a good few weeks for the whole process to complete.

It's essential that your existing savings do not lose their tax-free status during the transfer process. Your ISA must therefore be transferred *directly* between the two managers.

You cannot personally cash in your existing ISA and hand the money over to a new provider. If you do, you will only be able to reinvest up to £7,000 – the annual maximum.

The easiest long-term fix is to invest through an ISA supermarket which will let you pick and choose between hundreds of investment funds from different fund managers. ISA supermarkets let you switch funds quickly and cheaply.

Can I transfer shares from a share option scheme into an ISA?

Employees who receive shares from an Inland Revenue approved share option scheme can transfer them into an ISA. Transfers must take place within 90 days of the stock leaving the approved scheme.

What happens to ISA income?

Outside an ISA, interest income is usually taxed at either 20% or 40% depending on whether you are a basic-rate taxpayer or a higher-rate taxpayer. Similarly any cash dividends you receive are taxed at either 0% (basic-rate taxpayers) or 25% (higher-rate taxpayers).

ISA income is completely tax free whether it is re-invested or paid out. If there is any tax due from gilt interest payments this can be reclaimed from the Inland Revenue and added to your account.

Can I withdraw money from my ISA?

What makes ISAs so attractive to many investors is their flexibility. You can take out some or all of your money at any time and no tax is payable.

However, some cash ISA providers may insist that you invest for a fixed period or require notice before you withdraw your money. You may lose some interest if you withdraw early.

If you take money out, any that you put back later will count against your current year's ISA allowance.

Example

Jo opens a cash ISA with £2,500. A few weeks later she withdraws £2,000. Later in the same year, Jo decides to replace the money by putting new funds into the account. However, she can only replace £500 because the annual investment limit for a cash ISA is £3,000 per tax year.

Can I borrow against my ISAs?

No. You must always remain the beneficial owner of your ISA investments. They may not be used as security for a loan.

What happens if I leave the UK?

If you start an ISA in the UK and then move abroad, you cannot continue putting money into an ISA (unless you are a Crown employee working overseas or married to one).

You can, however, keep your existing ISAs and, when you return, you can start investing again.

Conclusion

Hopefully having read the above sections you'll have a good understanding of the various rules and regulations governing the ISA tax shelter.

They're not very complicated investments. You can invest up to a certain annual maximum and all your returns are tax free and instantly available for withdrawal. There's not much more to it than that.

What is a bit more complicated is working out how to maximise your ISA tax savings. Get it right and you'll save thousands in tax in the years ahead. Get it wrong and you'll be squandering a precious tax break.

Need Affordable & Expert Tax Planning Help?

Try Our Unique Question & Answer Service

Taxcafe.co.uk has a unique online tax help service that provides access to highly qualified tax professionals at an affordable rate.

No matter how complex your question, we will provide you with detailed tax planning guidance through this service. The cost is just £69.95.

To find out more go to **www.taxcafe.co.uk** and click the Tax Questions button.

Pay Less Tax!

... with help from Taxcafe's unique tax guides, software

All products available online at www.taxcafe.co.uk

➢ **How to Avoid Property Tax** - Essential reading for property investors who want to know all the tips and tricks to follow to pay less tax on their property profits.

➢ **Non Resident & Offshore Tax Planning** - How to exploit non-resident tax status to reduce your tax bill, plus advice on using offshore trusts and companies.

➢ **Using a Property Company to Save Tax** - How to massively increase your profits by using a property company... plus all the traps to avoid.

➢ **How to Avoid Inheritance Tax** - A-Z of inheritance tax planning, with clear explanations and numerous examples. Covers simple and sophisticated tax planning.

➢ **How to Avoid Stamp Duty** - Little known but perfectly legal trade secrets to reduce your stamp duty bill when buying or selling property.

➢ **Grow Rich with a Property ISA** - Find out how to invest in property tax free with an ISA.

➢ **Using a Company to Save Tax** - Everything you need to know about the tax benefits of using a company to run your business.

➢ **Bonus vs Dividend** - Shows how shareholder/directors of companies can save thousands in tax by choosing the optimal mix of bonus and dividend.

- ➤ **How to Avoid Tax on Your Stock Market Profits** - How to pay less capital gains tax, income tax and inheritance tax on your stock market investments and dealings.

- ➤ **Selling a Sole Trader Business** - A potential minefield with numerous traps to avoid but significant tax-saving opportunities.

- ➤ **How to Claim Tax Credits** - Even families with higher incomes can make successful tax credit claims. This guide shows how much you can claim and how to go about it.

- ➤ **Property Capital Gains Tax Calculator** - Unique software that performs complex capital gains tax calculations in seconds.

Disclaimer

1. Please note that this Tax Guide is intended as general guidance only for individual readers and does NOT constitute accountancy, tax, investment or other professional advice. Taxcafe UK Limited accepts no responsibility or liability for loss which may arise from reliance on information contained in this Tax Guide.

2. Please note that tax legislation, the law and practices by government and regulatory authorities (eg Inland Revenue) are constantly changing and the information contained in this Tax Guide is only correct as at the date of publication. We therefore recommend that for accountancy, tax, investment or other professional advice, you consult a suitably qualified accountant, tax specialist, independent financial adviser, or other professional adviser. Please also note that your personal circumstances may vary from the general examples given in this Tax Guide and your professional adviser will be able to give specific advice based on your personal circumstances.

3. This Tax Guide covers UK taxation only and any references to "tax" or "taxation" in this Tax Guide, unless the contrary is expressly stated, refers to UK taxation only. Please note that references to the "UK" do not include the Channel Islands or the Isle of Man. Foreign tax implications are beyond the scope of this Tax Guide.

4. Whilst in an effort to be helpful, this Tax Guide may refer to general guidance on matters other than UK taxation. Taxcafe UK Limited does not accept any responsibility or liability for loss which may arise from reliance on such information contained in this Tax Guide.

Printed in the United Kingdom
by Lightning Source UK Ltd.
109375UKS00001B/1-99